The Idea of
Spatial Form

The Idea

of

Spatial Form

JOSEPH FRANK

RUTGERS UNIVERSITY PRESS

New Brunswick and London

Library of Congress Cataloging-in-Publication Data

Frank, Joseph, 1918–
    The idea of spatial form.
Joseph Frank.
        p.   cm.
    Includes bibliographical references.
    ISBN 0-8135-1633-1 (cloth)   ISBN 0-8135-1643-9 (pbk.)
    1. Literature, Modern—20th century—History and criticism.
    2. Art, Modern—20th century. I. Title.
    PN771.F69   1991
    809'.04—dc20   90-8772
                                                                              CIP

British Cataloging-in-Publication information available

Essays in this book have been previously published, in different form, in
the following journals.
"Spatial Form in Modern Literature," *Sewanee Review* 53 (Spring, Sum-
    mer, Autumn 1945).
"Spatial Form: An Answer to Critics," *Critical Inquiry* 4 (Winter 1977).
"Spatial Form: Some Further Reflections," *Critical Inquiry* 5 (1978).
"André Malraux: A Metaphysics of Modern Art," *Partisan Review* (Febru-
    ary 1950).
"Formal Criticism and Abstract Art," *Hudson Review* (Spring 1954).
"E. H. Gombrich: The Language of Art," *Minnesota Review* (Spring 1961).

This volume is dedicated to the memory of
Allen Tate (1899–1979)
poet, novelist, critic, biographer, man of letters
with gratitude and admiration

Contents

.5.

.6.

Preface

The present volume of essays was conceived, initially, as a means of getting everything I had written on the question of spatial form between the covers of one book. My original essay, "Spatial Form in Modern Literature," was published in *Sewanee Review* in 1945; sections of the text then appeared in various anthologies of criticism; and it was reprinted in full, with some slight changes, in my first volume of essays, *The Widening Gyre* (1963). This volume is out of print, and so is the paperback edition published in 1968. It therefore seemed a good idea to make it available again.

All the more so because, thirty years after writing it and when my energies had become absorbed by a quite different field of study (Dostoevsky and the history of Russian literature and culture), I decided to return to my youthful interest in modernism and take up once again, in the light of more recent developments, some of the issues broached in the article and in the gratifyingly large discussion it had elicited.[1] My decision to do so arose out of a specific event that I cannot resist recalling at this point, which made me realize to what extent my ideas, with whose repercussions I had more or less lost contact, were still attracting attention and provoking controversy.

I believe it was in 1975 or 1976 that I received an invitation to participate in a session at the annual meeting of the Modern Language Association devoted to spatial form. The meeting was to take place in New York, I was then teaching in Princeton, and I decided to attend out of curiosity. Arriving a bit late, and quite surprised to find the room full and all the seats taken, I stood in the doorway for a good hour listening to the proceedings. The papers led to many questions about my ideas, and some participants speculated about what I had left unsaid (bringing up matters that, in truth, I had never thought about at all). One of the queries that kept recurring was why I had never written a word of response to all the criticisms that had been leveled at my theories and analyses. The real answer, aside from my innate aversion to literary polemics (I am always overcome by a depressing sense of tedium and futility whenever I read any), was simply that the focus of my studies had turned elsewhere. But I felt a little like a ghost returning to visit his former life and learning of everything he had neglected to do while on earth. I decided then and there to take the time to read through this material and see what could be said to answer the inquiries of those who were interested in my reflections. Initially, I thought I would only reply to my critics; but this hardly seemed worth doing by itself, and so I was led to reexamine my ideas in the light of theories I had been unfamiliar with earlier (such as Russian Formalism), or which had emerged later.

All this occurred fourteen years ago, and in view of the present ferment in literary theory and criticism one may well doubt that such a notion as spatial form, now more than half a century old, still has any relevance to contemporary concerns. If we are to judge the vitality of an idea by the frequency with which it is attacked, how-

ever, then spatial form, I am happy to say, still has not
been relegated to the dustbin of history. Just as this
book was going to press, I came across another side-
swipe at it in the course of a rather rambling but touching tribute paid by Richard Poirier to his old teachers at
Amherst. They were, it seems, far superior to the much
better known New Critics reigning at Yale and Vander-
bilt, who are piously denounced in ritual fashion. This
is not the place to argue the merits of this critical mantra
any further, but it appears that my essay is, as it were,
the concentrated essence of the noxious New Critical influence on the study of literature.

As Poirier sees it, the incalculable damage that the
New Critics and Eliot, with his "mythic method," have
done to the reading of literature both new and old "is
epitomized in such influential codifications as Joseph
Frank's essay of 1945 . . . where it is proposed that Eliot,
Pound, Proust, Joyce, and Djuna Barnes 'ideally intend
the reader to apprehend their works spatially, in a moment of time, rather than as a sequence.'" Hastening to
the barricades, the vigilant critic retorts that reading "is
an experience in time and not in space; we read, we
know 'what it is like to read,' in sequence."[2] Indeed we
do; and by the word "ideally" in the above quotation, I
indicated my awareness that the intention mentioned
cannot ever be fully realized precisely because reading is
"an experience in time." But a good deal of modern
literature makes no sense if read *only* as a sequence, and
it was the implications of this self-evident anomaly that I
wished to examine. Many people have assured me over
the years that my explorations have been very helpful
for *their* reading, and I can only leave it to the future to
decide whether this will continue to be the case.

It would seem, then, that my theory of spatial form

has by no means as yet lost its capacity to stimulate response, whether approval or contestation; and I am
happy to record an instance of the former coming from a
totally unexpected quarter. A recent Russian anthology of Western literary criticism of the nineteenth and
twentieth centuries, whose sixteen entries range from
Sainte-Beuve and Taine to Dilthy, Heidegger, Sartre, and
Northrop Frye, also contains a translation of the short-
ened form of my article prepared for Mark Schorer's
1948 collection.[4] It thus occurred to me that a few words
about its origins might be of some general interest. The
work originated in my fascination with Djuna Barnes's
Nightwood, which I read shortly after its publication in
1937. The book haunted me for some reason, and I began trying to define for myself the difference between it
and more conventional novels, even though it was not
as obviously experimental as, say, *Ulysses* or some early
Faulkner. I was struck by T. S. Eliot's comparison in
the preface between the prose of the novel and poetry,
which led me to see if I could pin down this observation
more concretely. My preoccupation was never abstract
or theoretical; I only wished to say something enlightening about a particular work. I did not set out to write a
theory of modern literature, and the notion that I might
be engaged in doing so, given my sense of my general
ignorance, never crossed my mind.

This explains the somewhat lopsided character of the
essay as a whole, which I am sure must have struck
a good many readers. Works of such great scope as
Ulysses and *Remembrance of Things Past* are passed by
very rapidly, while *Nightwood* receives a far more extensive treatment. Part of the reason is that much work on
Joyce and Proust had already been done, and I was not
out to compete with it; part is simply that, even when

my original intention had greatly expanded, I still remained attached to my initial purpose. Possibly out of a sense of gratitude to the book that had started me on the way, and had received very little attention, I insisted on giving *Nightwood* a place of honor.

For a number of years after reading *Nightwood*, I thought about some of the questions it raised and jotted down quotations from my reading. Most were later incorporated into the text, but I did not find a place for others. I distinctly recall, for example, writing down the famous passage from G. Wilson Knight's *The Wheel of Fire* (which several commentators have rightly spotted as related to my point of view) in which he asserts that "a Shakespearian tragedy is set spatially as well as temporally in the mind," and that there are in the plays "a set of correspondences which are related to each other independently of the time-sequence of the story." I also remember reading, with great admiration, an essay on Virginia Woolf by William Troy (one of the best and most original critics of his generation, now unjustly forgotten) who noted how Woolf's symbolic structures contradicted the laws of narrative. Taking down his *Selected Essays* from the shelf, I discover: "The symbol may be considered as something *spatial*" (italics in original); and the further remark that in poetry, "whether separate or integrated into a total vision, symbols are capable of being grasped, like other aspects of space, by a single and instantaneous effort of perception."

Suggestions of this kind no doubt came pouring in from all directions; but I really did not know how to use these hints and pointers for a long time.[3] It was only, I believe, when I began to think along the lines of a comparison of literature and the visual arts that matters began to become somewhat clearer. I had read a good bit of art criticism earlier—Roger Fry, Clive Bell, Herbert Read—and had studied modern art with Meyer Schapiro at the New School for Social Research in the mid-1930s. Heinrich Wölfflin certainly taught me something about the possibilities of formal analysis; and I was led to Wilhelm Worringer by his influence on T. E. Hulme and the constant references to him in English criticism. But I recall vividly that my ideas only began to take coherent shape once I finally read Lessing's *Laocoön,* which I may have been led to because of the discussion of time and space in Edwin Muir's classic *Structure of the Novel.*

I have a distinct recollection of the exhilaration I felt after going through Lessing in the little Everyman edition, whose rippled crimson cover I can still feel in my hands and see before my eyes. Here was the systematic clue I had been searching for without knowing it. And I only began to write seriously and stubbornly after this discovery, now that I knew what I was doing and had something to say I had found nowhere else among the critics I had read and from whom I had learned.

Some years later, through a stroke of luck, the first part of the still unfinished essay was shown by a mutual friend to Allen Tate; and he called me from his office in the Library of Congress (I was then working as a journalist in Washington, D.C.) to invite me for lunch. I shall never forget his interest and encouragement, or his insistence that I hurry and complete the continuation I sketched for him so that he could use the essay for *Sewanee Review,* whose editorship he was soon to assume. The dedication of the present volume to his memory is only a small acknowledgment of all my indebtedness to him for his continuing kindness and unfailing friendship from that time on.

It was only after several years, in 1948 to be exact, that the publication of parts of the essay in an anthology of criticism edited by Mark Schorer brought it to the attention of a wider audience and really launched it on its career. Shortly after the first periodical installment had appeared, however, I received a call from New York asking for the right to translate a condensed version of the entire text into Spanish. The caller was the editor of *La Revista Belga*, a monthly journal financed at that time by the Belgian government and intended for Latin American readers. Naturally, I was very pleased and hastened to agree; if my memory is correct, the last part of the essay appeared in Spanish even *before* it was printed in English. I have often wondered who read it, and whether it came to the attention of any of the younger Latin American novelists who seem to exemplify its principles so well.

The present volume also includes three other essays that, in my own mind, are linked with some of the questions raised in my spatial form article and written as offshoots and extrapolations of its ideas. All are concerned with the larger issues of modern art and modernism touched on in sections VI and VII; all focus on problems arising from the same mutation in Western culture that gave rise to spatial form. My article on André Malraux's *The Psychology of Art* is earlier than the one on *The Voices of Silence* published in *The Widening Gyre;* and though there is some similarity between them, there are also enough differences to justify the reappearance of this first reaction to a superb work (or series of works) whose present neglect by specialists is no gauge of their true stature. I was pleased to be able to record the revision by E. H. Gombrich of his initial, all too influential, totally negative appraisal.

All the essays are printed substantially unchanged, except for some slight modifications, but with the addition of notes and two postscripts that take account of

other or more recent opinions. I should like to thank
Leslie Mitchner of Rutgers Press for her backing and aid
with this project. Most of all, though, my thanks go
once again to my wife Marguerite, who insisted for
many years that a small book on spatial form was desirable and feasible even when prospective publishers
thought it impractical. The present edition would not
have come into being without her belief in its possibility.

JOSEPH FRANK
Paris, France, May 1990

Notes

1. For a bibliography of works concerned with spatial
   form, see *Spatial Form in Narrative,* ed. Jeffrey R.
   Smitten and Ann Daghistany (Ithaca and London,
   1981), 245–263.
2. Richard Poirier, "Hum 6, or Reading before Theory," *Raritan Review* 9 (Spring 1990), 26.
3. An extremely informative analysis of the general
   cultural background can be found in James M. Cur-
   tis, "Spatial Form in the Context of Modernist Aesthetics," in *Spatial Form in Narrative,* ed. Smitten and
   Daghistany, 161–178. An excellent reconstruction
   of the literary-critical situation can be found in chapter 3 of Ronald Foust, "The Place of Spatial Form in
   Modern Literary Criticism" (Ph.D. diss., University
   of Maryland, 1975).
4. *Zarubezhnaya Estetika i Teoriya Literaturi xix-xx vv.,*
   ed. G. K. Kosikov (Moscow, 1987). I am greatly in-
   debted to my colleague Lazar Fleishman, who returned from the Soviet Union with a copy of this
   book and called it to my attention just in time to be
   mentioned here.

The Idea of
Spatial Form

1

*S*patial Form in
Modern Literature

I. Introduction

"Lessing's *Laocoön*," André Gide once remarked, "is one of those books it is good to reiterate or contradict every thirty years."[1] Despite this excellent advice, neither of these attitudes toward *Laocoön* has been adopted by modern writers. Lessing's attempt to define the limits of literature and the plastic arts has become a dead issue; it is neither reiterated nor contradicted but simply neglected. Lessing, to be sure, occupies an honorable place in the history of criticism and aesthetics. But while his work is invariably referred to with respect, it can hardly be said to have exercised any fecundating influence on modern aesthetic thinking,[2] This was comprehensible enough in the nineteenth century, with its overriding passion for historicism; but it is not so easy to understand at present when so many writers on aesthetic problems are occupied with questions of form. To a historian of literature or the plastic arts, Lessing's effort to define the unalterable laws of these mediums may well have seemed quixotic. Modern critics, however, no longer overawed by the bugbear of historical method, have begun to take up again the problems he tried to solve.

Lessing's own solution to these problems seems at first glance to have little relation to modern concerns. The literary school against which the arguments of *Laocoön* were directed—the school of pictorial poetry— has long since ceased to interest the modern sensibility.

Many of Lessing's conclusions grew out of a now anti-quated archaeology, whose discoveries, to make matters worse, he knew mainly at second hand. But it was pre-cisely his attempt to rise above history, to define the un-alterable laws of aesthetic perception rather than to attack or defend any particular school, that gives his work the perennial freshness to which André Gide al-luded. The validity of his theories does not depend on their relationship to the literary movements of his time or on the extent of his firsthand acquaintanceship with the art works of antiquity. It is thus always possible to consider them apart from these circumstances and to use them in the analysis of later developments.

In *Laocoön* Lessing fuses two distinct currents of thought, both of great importance in the cultural history of his time. The archaeological researches of his contem-porary Winckelmann had stimulated a passionate inter-est in Greek culture among the Germans. Lessing went back to Homer, Aristotle, and the Greek tragedians and, using his firsthand knowledge, attacked the distorted critical theories (supposedly based on classical author-ity) that had filtered into France through Italian com-mentators and had then taken hold in Germany.

At the same time Locke and the empirical school of English philosophy had given a new impulse to aes-thetic speculation. For Locke tried to solve the problem of knowledge by breaking down complex ideas into simple elements of sensation and then examining the operations of the mind to see how these sensations were combined to form ideas. This method was soon taken over by aestheticians, whose focus of interest shifted from external prescriptions for beauty to an analysis of aesthetic perception; and writers like Shaftesbury, Ho-garth, Hutcheson, and Burke concerned themselves with the precise character and combination of impressions that gave aesthetic pleasure to the sensibility. Lessing's friend and critical ally Mendelssohn popularized this method of dealing with aesthetic problems in German; and Lessing himself was a close student of all the works of this school. As a result, *Laocoön* stands at the confluence of these intellectual currents. Lessing analyzes the laws of aesthetic perception, shows how they prescribe necessary limitations to literature and the plastic arts, and then demonstrates how Greek writers and painters, especially his cherished Homer, created masterpieces in obedience to these laws.

Lessing's argument starts from the simple observation that literature and the plastic arts, working through different sensuous mediums, must differ in the fundamental laws governing their creation. "If it is true," Lessing wrote in *Laocoön*, "that painting and poetry in their imitations make use of entirely different means or symbols—the first, namely, of form and color in space, the second of articulated sounds in time—if these symbols indisputably require a suitable relation to the thing symbolized, then it is clear that symbols arranged in juxtaposition can only express subjects of which the wholes or parts exist in juxtaposition; while consecutive symbols can only express subjects of which the wholes or parts are themselves consecutive."

Lessing did not originate this formulation, which has a long and complicated history; but he was the first to use it systematically as an instrument of critical analysis. Form in the plastic arts, according to Lessing, is necessarily spatial because the visible aspect of objects can best be presented juxtaposed in an instant of time. Literature, on the other hand, makes use of language, composed of a succession of words proceeding through time; and it follows that literary form, to harmonize with the essential quality of its medium, must be based primarily on some form of narrative sequence.

Lessing used this argument to attack two artistic genres highly popular in his day: pictorial poetry and allegorical painting. The pictorial poet tried to paint with words; the allegorical painter to tell a story in visible images. Both were doomed to fail because their aims were in contradiction to the fundamental properties of their mediums. No matter how accurate and vivid a verbal description might be, Lessing argued, it could not give the unified impression of a visible object. No matter how skillfully figures might be chosen and arranged, a painting or a piece of sculpture could not successfully set forth the various stages of an action.

As Lessing develops his argument, he attempts to prove that the Greeks, with an unfailing sense of aesthetic propriety, respected the limits imposed on different art mediums by the conditions of human perception. The importance of Lessing's distinction, however, does not depend on these ramifications of his argument, nor even on his specific critical judgments. Various critics have quarreled with one or another of these judgments and have thought this sufficient to undermine Lessing's position; but such a notion is based on a misunderstanding of *Laocoön*'s importance in the history of aesthetic theory. It is quite possible to use Lessing's insights solely as instruments of analysis, without proceeding to judge the value of individual works by how closely they adhere to the norms he laid down; and unless this is done, as a matter of fact, the real meaning of *Laocoön* cannot be understood. For what Lessing offered was not a new set of norms but a new approach to aesthetic form.

The conception of aesthetic form inherited by the

eighteenth century from the Renaissance was purely external. Greek and Roman literature—or what was known of it—was presumed to have reached perfection, and later writers could do little better than imitate its example. A horde of commentators and critics had deduced certain rules from the classical masterpieces (rules like the Aristotelian unities, of which Aristotle had never heard), and modern writers were warned to obey these rules if they wished to appeal to a cultivated public. Gradually, these rules became an immutable mold into which the material of a literary work had to be poured: the form of a work was nothing but the technical arrangement dictated by the rules. Such a superficial and mechanical notion of aesthetic form, however, led to serious perversions of taste—Shakespeare was considered a barbarian even by so sophisticated a writer as Voltaire, and, in translating Homer, Pope found it necessary to do a good deal of editing. Lessing's point of view, breaking sharply with this external conception of form, marks the road for aesthetic speculation to follow in the future.

For Lessing, as we have seen, aesthetic form is not an external arrangement provided by a set of traditional rules. Rather, it is the relation between the sensuous nature of the art medium and the conditions of human perception. The "natural man" of the eighteenth century was not to be bound by traditional political forms but was to create them in accordance with his own nature. Similarly, art was to create its own forms out of itself rather than accept them ready-made from the practice of the past; and criticism, instead of prescribing rules for art, was to explore the necessary laws by which art governs itself.

No longer was aesthetic form confused with mere externals of technique or felt as a strait jacket into which the artist, willy-nilly, had to force his creative ideas. Form issued spontaneously from the organization of the art work as it presented itself to perception. Time and space were the two extremes defining the limits of literature and the plastic arts in their relation to sensuous perception; and, following Lessing's example, it is possible to trace the evolution of art forms by their oscillations between these two poles.

The purpose of the present essay is to apply Lessing's method to modern literature—to trace the evolution of form in modern poetry and, more particularly, in the novel. For modern literature, as exemplified by such writers as T. S. Eliot, Ezra Pound, Marcel Proust, and James Joyce, is moving in the direction of spatial form; and this tendency receives an original development in Djuna Barnes's remarkable book *Nightwood*. All these writers ideally intend the reader to apprehend their work spatially, in a moment of time, rather than as a sequence. And since changes in aesthetic form always involve major changes in the sensibility of a particular cultural period, an effort will be made to outline the spiritual attitudes that have led to the predominance of spatial form.

II. Modern Poetry

Modern Anglo-American poetry received its initial impetus from the Imagist movement of the years directly preceding and following the First World War. Imagism was important not so much for any actual poetry written by Imagist poets—no one knew quite what an Imagist poet was—but rather because it opened the way for later developments by its clean break with sentimental

Victorian verbiage. The critical writings of Ezra Pound, the leading theoretician of Imagism, are an astonishing farrago of acute aesthetic perceptions thrown in among a series of boyishly naughty remarks whose chief purpose is to *épater le bourgeois*. But Pound's definition of the image, perhaps the keenest of his perceptions, is of fundamental importance for any discussion of modern literary form. "An 'Image,'" Pound wrote, "is that which presents an intellectual and emotional complex in an instant of time." The implications of this definition should be noted: an image is defined not as a pictorial reproduction but as a unification of disparate ideas and emotions into a complex presented spatially in an instant of time. Such a complex does not proceed discursively, in unison with the laws of language, but strikes the reader's sensibility with an instantaneous impact. Pound stresses this aspect by adding, in the next paragraph, that only the *instantaneous* presentation of such complexes gives "that sense of sudden liberation; that sense of freedom from time limits and space limits; that sense of sudden growth, which we experience in the presence of the greatest works of art."[3]

At the very outset, therefore, modern poetry advocates a poetic method in direct contradiction to Lessing's analysis of language. And if we compare Pound's definition of the image with Eliot's description of the psychology of the poetic process, we can see clearly how profoundly this conception has influenced our modern idea of the nature of poetry. For Eliot, the distinctive quality of a poetic sensibility is its capacity to form new wholes, to fuse seemingly disparate experiences into an organic unity. The ordinary man, Eliot writes, "falls in love, or reads Spinoza, and these two experiences have nothing to do with each other, or with the noise of the typewriter or the smell of cooking; in the mind of the poet these experiences are always forming new wholes."[4] Pound had attempted to define the image in terms of its aesthetic attributes; Eliot, in this passage, is describing its psychological origin; but the result in a poem would be the same in both cases.

Such a view of the nature of poetry immediately gave rise to numerous problems. How was more than one image to be included in a poem? If the chief value of an image was its capacity to present an intellectual and emotional complex simultaneously, linking images in a sequence would clearly destroy most of their efficacy. Or was the poem itself one vast image, whose individual components were to be apprehended as a unity? But then it would be necessary to undermine the inherent consecutiveness of language, frustrating the reader's normal expectation of a sequence and forcing him to perceive the elements of the poem as juxtaposed in space rather than unrolling in time.

This is precisely what Eliot and Pound attempted in their major works. Both poets, in their earlier work, had still retained some elements of conventional structure. Their poems were looked upon as daring and revolutionary chiefly because of technical matters, like the loosening of metrical pattern and the handling of subjects ordinarily considered nonpoetic. Perhaps this is less true of Eliot than of Pound, especially the Eliot of the more complex early works like *Prufrock*, *Gerontion* and *Portrait of a Lady*; but even here, although the sections of the poem are not governed by syntactical logic, the skeleton of an implied narrative structure is always present. The reader of *Prufrock* is swept up in a narrative movement from the very first lines:

Let us go then, you and I,
When the evening . . .

And the reader, accompanying Prufrock, finally arrives at their mutual destination:

In the room the women come and go
Talking of Michelangelo.

At this point the poem becomes a series of more or less isolated fragments, each stating some aspect of Prufrock's emotional dilemma. But the fragments are now localized and focused on a specific set of circumstances, and the reader can organize them by referring to the implied situation. The same method is employed in *Portrait of a Lady*, while in *Gerontion* the reader is specifically told that he has been reading the "thoughts of a dry brain in a dry season"—the stream of consciousness of "an old man in a dry month, being read to by a boy, waiting for the rain." In both poems there is a perceptible framework around which the seemingly disconnected passages of the poem can be organized.

This is one reason why Pound's *Mauberley* and Eliot's early work were first regarded, not as forerunners of a new poetic form, but as latter-day *vers de société*—witty, disillusioned, with a somewhat brittle charm, but lacking that quality of "high seriousness" which Matthew Arnold had brandished as the touchstone of poetic excellence. These poems were considered unusual mainly because *vers de société* had long fallen out of fashion, but there was little difficulty in accepting them as an entertaining departure from the grand style of the nineteenth century.

In the *Cantos* and *The Waste Land*, however, it should have been clear that a radical transformation was taking place in aesthetic structure; but this transformation has been touched on only peripherally by modern critics. R. P. Blackmur comes closest to the central problem while analyzing what he calls Pound's "anecdotal" method. The special form of the *Cantos*, Blackmur explains, "is that of the anecdote begun in one place, taken up in one or more other places, and finished, if at all, in still another. This deliberate disconnectedness, this art of a thing continually alluding to itself, continually breaking off short, is the method by which the *Cantos* tie themselves together. So soon as the reader's mind is concerted with the material of the poem, Mr. Pound deliberately disconcerts it, either by introducing fresh and disjunct material or by reverting to old and, apparently, equally disjunct material."[5]

Blackmur's remarks apply equally well to *The Waste Land*, where syntactical sequence is given up for a structure depending on the perception of relationships between disconnected word-groups. To be properly understood, these word-groups must be juxtaposed with one another and perceived simultaneously. Only when this is done can they be adequately grasped; for, while they follow one another in time, their meaning does not depend on this temporal relationship. The one difficulty of these poems, which no amount of textual exegesis can wholly overcome, is the internal conflict between the time-logic of language and the space-logic implicit in the modern conception of the nature of poetry.

Aesthetic form in modern poetry, then, is based on a space-logic that demands a complete reorientation in the reader's attitude toward language. Since the primary reference of any word-group is to something inside the poem itself, language in modern poetry is really reflexive. The meaning-relationship is completed only by the simultaneous perception in space of word-groups that have no comprehensible relation to each other when read consecutively in time. Instead of the instinctive and immediate reference of words and word-groups to the objects or events they symbolize and the construction of meaning from the sequence of these references, modern poetry asks its readers to suspend the process of individual reference temporarily until the entire pattern of internal references can be apprehended as a unity.

It would not be difficult to trace this conception of poetic form back to Mallarmé's ambition to create a language of "absence" rather than of presence—a language in which words negated their objects instead of designating them;[6] nor should one overlook the evident formal analogies between *The Waste Land* and the *Cantos* and Mallarmé's *Un Coup de dés*. Mallarmé, indeed, dislocated the temporality of language far more radically than either Eliot or Pound has ever done; and his experience with *Un Coup de dés* showed that this ambition of modern poetry has a necessary limit. If pursued with Mallarmé's relentlessness, it culminates in the self-negation of language and the creation of a hybrid pictographic "poem" that can only be considered a fascinating historical curiosity. Nonetheless, this conception of aesthetic form, which may be formulated as the principle of reflexive reference, has left its traces on all of modern poetry. And the principle of reflexive reference is the link connecting the aesthetic development of modern poetry with similar experiments in the modern novel.

III. Flaubert and Joyce

For a study of aesthetic form in the modern novel, Flaubert's famous county fair scene in *Madame Bovary* is a convenient point of departure. This scene has been justly praised for its mordant caricature of bourgeois pomposity, its portrayal—unusually sympathetic for Flaubert—of the bewildered old servant, and its burlesque of the pseudoromantic rhetoric by which Rodolphe woos the sentimental Emma. At present, however, it is enough to notice the method by which Flaubert handles the scene—a method we might as well call cinematographic since this analogy comes immediately to mind.

As Flaubert sets the scene, there is action going on simultaneously at three levels; and the physical position of each level is a fair index to its spiritual significance. On the lowest plane, there is the surging, jostling mob in the street, mingling with the livestock brought to the exhibitions. Raised slightly above the street by a platform are the speechmaking officials, bombastically reeling off platitudes to the attentive multitudes. And on the highest level of all, from a window overlooking the spectacle, Rodolphe and Emma are watching the proceedings and carrying on their amorous conversation in phrases as stilted as those regaling the crowds. Albert Thibaudet has compared this scene to the medieval mystery play, in which various related actions occur simultaneously on different stage levels;[7] but this acute comparison refers to Flaubert's intention rather than to his method. *"Everything should sound simultaneously,"* Flaubert later wrote, in commenting on this scene; "one should hear the bellowing of cattle, the whispering of the lovers, and the rhetoric of the officials all at the same time."[8]

But since language proceeds in time, it is impossible to approach this simultaneity of perception except by breaking up temporal sequence. And this is exactly what Flaubert does. He dissolves sequence by cutting back and forth between the various levels of action in a slowly rising crescendo until—at the climax of the scene —Rodolphe's Chateaubriandesque phrases are read at almost the same moment as the names of prize winners for raising the best pigs. Flaubert takes care to underline this satiric similarity by exposition as well as by juxtaposition—as if afraid the reflexive relations of the two actions might not be grasped: "From magnetism, by slow degrees, Rodolphe had arrived at affinities, and while M. le Président was citing Cincinnatus at his plow, Diocletian planting his cabbages and the emperors of China ushering in the new year with sowing-festivals, the young man was explaining to the young woman that these irresistible attractions sprang from some anterior existence."

This scene illustrates, on a small scale, what we mean by the spatialization of form in a novel. For the duration of the scene, at least, the time-flow of the narrative is halted; attention is fixed on the interplay of relationships within the immobilized time-area. These relationships are juxtaposed independently of the progress of the narrative, and the full significance of the scene is given only by the reflexive relations among the units of meaning. In Flaubert's scene, however, the unit of meaning is not, as in modern poetry, a word-group or a fragment of an anecdote; it is the totality of each level of action taken as an integer. The unit is so large that each

integer can be read with an illusion of complete understanding, yet with a total unawareness of what Thibaudet calls the "dialectic of platitude" interweaving all
levels and finally linking them together with devastating
irony.

In other words, the adoption of spatial form in Pound
and Eliot resulted in the disappearance of coherent sequence after a few lines; but the novel, with its larger
unit of meaning, can preserve coherent sequence within
the unit of meaning and break up only the time-flow of
narrative. Because of this difference readers of modern
poetry are practically forced to read reflexively to get
any literal sense, while readers of a novel like *Nightwood*, for example, are led to expect narrative sequence
by the deceptive normality of language sequence within
the unit of meaning. But this does not affect the parallel
between aesthetic form in modern poetry and the form
of Flaubert's scene. Both can be properly understood
only when their units of meaning are apprehended reflexively in an instant of time.

Flaubert's scene, although interesting in itself, is of
minor importance to his novel as a whole and is skillfully blended back into the main narrative structure
after fulfilling its satiric function. But Flaubert's method
was taken over by James Joyce and applied on a gigantic
scale in the composition of *Ulysses*. Joyce composed his
novel of a vast number of references and cross references that relate to each other independently of the time
sequence of the narrative. These references must be
connected by the reader and viewed as a whole before
the book fits together into any meaningful pattern. Ultimately, if we are to believe Stuart Gilbert, these systems
of reference form a complete picture of practically everything under the sun, from the stages of man's life

and the organs of the human body to the colors of the spectrum; but these structures are far more important for Joyce, as Harry Levin has remarked, than they could ever possibly be for the reader.[9] And while students of Joyce, fascinated by his erudition, have usually applied themselves to exegesis, our problem is to inquire into the perceptual form of his novel.

Joyce's most obvious intention in *Ulysses* is to give the reader a picture of Dublin seen as a whole—to re-create the sights and sounds, the people and places, of a typical Dublin day, much as Flaubert had re-created his *comice agricole*. And like Flaubert, Joyce aimed at attaining the same unified impact, the same sense of simultaneous activity occurring in different places. As a matter of fact, Joyce frequently makes use of the same method as Flaubert (cutting back and forth between different actions occurring at the same time), and he usually does so to obtain the same ironic effect. But Joyce faced the additional problem of creating this impression of simultaneity for the life of a whole teeming city and of maintaining it—or rather of strengthening it—through hundreds of pages that must be read as a sequence. To meet this problem Joyce was forced to go far beyond what Flaubert had done. Flaubert had still maintained a clear-cut narrative line except in the county fair scene; but Joyce breaks up his narrative and transforms the very structure of his novel into an instrument of his aesthetic intention.

Joyce conceived *Ulysses* as a modern epic. And in the epic, as Stephen Dedalus tells us in *A Portrait of the Artist as a Young Man*, "the personality of the artist, at first sight a cry or a cadence and then a fluid and lambent narrative, finally refines itself out of existence, impersonalizes itself, so to speak . . . the artist, like the

God of creation, remains within or beyond or above his handiwork, invisible, refined out of existence, indifferent, paring his finger-nails." The epic is thus synonymous for Joyce with the complete self-effacement of the author; and with his usual uncompromising rigor Joyce carries this implication further than anyone had previously dared.

For Joyce assumes—what is obviously not true—that all his readers are Dubliners, intimately acquainted with Dublin life and the personal history of his characters. This allows him to refrain from giving any direct information about his characters and thus betraying the presence of an omniscient author. What Joyce does, instead, is to present the elements of his narrative—the relations between Stephen and his family, between Bloom and his wife, between Stephen and Bloom and the Dedalus family—in fragments, as they are thrown out unexplained in the course of casual conversation or as they lie embedded in the various strata of symbolic reference. The same is true of all the allusions to Dublin life and history and to the external events of the twenty-four hours during which the novel takes place. All the factual background summarized for the reader in an ordinary novel must here be reconstructed from fragments, sometimes hundreds of pages apart, scattered through the book. As a result, the reader is forced to read *Ulysses* in exactly the same manner as he reads modern poetry, that is, by continually fitting fragments together and keeping allusions in mind until, by reflexive reference, he can link them to their complements.

Joyce desired in this way to build up in the reader's mind a sense of Dublin as a totality, including all the relations of the characters to one another and all the events that enter their consciousness. The reader is intended to acquire this sense as he progresses through the novel, connecting allusions and references spatially and gradually becoming aware of the pattern of relationships. At the conclusion it might almost be said that Joyce literally wanted the reader to become a Dubliner. For this is what Joyce demands: that the reader have at hand the same instinctive knowledge of Dublin life, the same sense of Dublin as a huge, surrounding organism, that the Dubliner possesses as a birthright. It is this birthright that, at any one moment of time, gives the native a knowledge of Dublin's past and present as a whole; and it is only such knowledge that would enable the reader, like the characters, to place all the references in their proper context. This, it should be realized, is the equivalent of saying that Joyce cannot be read—he can only be reread. A knowledge of the whole is essential to an understanding of any part; but unless one is a Dubliner such knowledge can be obtained only after the book has been read, when all the references are fitted into their proper places and grasped as a unity. The burdens placed on the reader by this method of composition may well seem insuperable. But the fact remains that Joyce, in his unbelievably laborious fragmentation of narrative structure, proceeded on the assumption that a unified spatial apprehension of his work would ultimately be possible.

IV. Proust

In a far more subtle manner than in either Joyce or Flaubert, the same principle of composition is at work in Marcel Proust. Since Proust himself tells us that his novel will have imprinted on it "a form which usually remains invisible, the form of Time," it may seem strange to speak of Proust in connection with spatial form. He has almost invariably been considered the novelist of time par excellence—the literary interpreter of that Bergsonian "real time" intuited by the sensibility, as distinguished from the abstract, chronological time of the conceptual intelligence. To stop at this point, however, is to miss what Proust himself considered the deepest significance of his work.

Oppressed and obsessed by a sense of the ineluctability of time and the evanescence of human life, Proust was suddenly, he tells us, visited by certain quasi-mystical experiences (described in detail in the last volume of his book, *Le Temps Retrouvé*). These experiences provided him with a spiritual technique for transcending time, and thus enabled him to escape time's domination. Proust believed that these transcendent, extratemporal moments contained a clue to the ultimate nature of reality; and he wished to translate these moments to the level of aesthetic form by writing a novel. But no ordinary narrative, which tried to convey their meaning indirectly through exposition and description, could really do them justice. For Proust desired, through the medium of his novel, to communicate to the reader the full impact of these moments as he had felt them himself.

To define the method by which this is accomplished, we must first understand clearly the precise nature of the Proustian revelation. Each such experience was marked by a feeling that "the permanent essence of things, usually concealed, is set free and our true self, which had long seemed dead but was not dead in other ways, awakes, takes on fresh life as it receives the celestial nourishment brought to it." This celestial nourishment consists of some sound, or odor, or other sensory stimulus, "sensed anew, simultaneously in the present and the past."

But why should these moments seem so overwhelmingly valuable that Proust calls them celestial? Because, Proust observes, imagination ordinarily can operate only on the past; the material presented to imagination thus lacks any sensuous immediacy. At certain moments, however, the physical sensations of the past come flooding back to fuse with the present; and Proust believed that in these moments he grasped a reality "real without being of the present moment, ideal but not abstract." Only in these moments did he attain his most cherished ambition—"to seize, isolate, immobilize for the duration of a lightning flash" what otherwise he could not apprehend, "namely: a fragment of time in its pure state." For a person experiencing this moment, Proust adds, the word "death" no longer has meaning. "Situated outside the scope of time, what could he fear from the future?"

The significance of this experience, though obscurely hinted at throughout the book, is made explicit only in the concluding pages, which describe the final appearance of the narrator at the reception of the Princesse de Guermantes. And the narrator decides to dedicate the remainder of his life to recreating these experiences in a work of art. This work will differ essentially from all others because, at its root, will be a vision of reality refracted through an extratemporal perspective. This decision, however, should not be confused with the Renaissance view of art as the guarantor of immortality, nor with the late nineteenth-century cult of art for art's sake (though Proust has obvious affinities with both traditions, and particularly with the latter). It was not the creation of a work of art per se that filled Proust with a sense of fulfilling a prophetic mission; it was the creation of a work of art that should stand as a monument to his *personal* conquest of time. His own novel was to be at once the vehicle through which he conveyed his vision and the *concrete experience* of that vision expressed in a form that compelled the world (the reader) to reexperience its exact effect on Proust's own sensibility.

The prototype of this method, like the analysis of the revelatory moment, appears during the reception at the Princesse de Guermantes's. The narrator has spent years in a sanatorium and has lost touch almost completely with the fashionable world of the earlier volumes; now he comes out of his seclusion to attend the reception. Accordingly, he finds himself bewildered by the changes in social position, and the even more striking changes in character and personality, among his former friends. No doubt these pages paint a striking picture of the invasion of French society by the upper bourgeoisie and the gradual breakdown of all social and moral standards caused by the First World War; but, as the narrator takes great pains to tell us, this is far from being the most important theme of this section of the book. Much more crucial is that, almost with the force of a blow, these changes jolt the narrator into a consciousness of the passage of time. He tries painfully to recognize old friends under the masks that, he feels, the years have welded to them. And when a young man addresses him respectfully instead of familiarly, he realizes suddenly that, without being aware of it, he too has assumed a mask— the mask of an elderly gentleman. The narrator now begins to understand that in order to become conscious of time it has been necessary for him to absent himself from his accustomed environment (in other words, from the stream of time acting on that environment) and then to plunge back into the stream again after a lapse of years. In so doing he finds himself presented with two images—the world as he had formerly known it and the world, transformed by time, that he now sees before him. When these two images become juxtaposed, the narrator discovers that the passage of time may suddenly be experienced through its visible effects.

Habit is a universal soporific, which ordinarily conceals the passage of time from those who have gone their accustomed ways. At any one moment of time the changes are so minute as to be imperceptible. "Other people," Proust writes, "never cease to change places in relation to ourselves. In the imperceptible, but eternal march of the world, we regard them as motionless in a moment of vision, too short for us to perceive the motion that is sweeping them on. But we have only to select in our memory two pictures taken of them at different moments, close enough together however for them not to have altered in themselves—perceptibly, that is to say—and the difference between the two pictures is a measure of the displacement that they have undergone in relation to us." By comparing these two images in a moment of time, the passage of time can be experienced concretely through the impact of its visible effects on the sensibility. And this discovery provides the narrator with a method that, in T. S. Eliot's phrase, is an "objective correlative" to the visionary apprehension of the fragment of "pure time" intuited in the revelatory moment.

When the narrator discovers this method of communicating his experience of the revelatory moment, he decides, as we have already observed, to incorporate it in a novel. But the novel the narrator undertakes to write has just been finished by the reader; and its form is controlled by the method that he has outlined in its concluding pages. In other words, the reader is substituted for the narrator and is placed by the author throughout the book in the same position as that occupied by the narrator before his own experience at the reception of the Princesse de Guermantes. This is done by the discontinuous presentation of character—a simple device which nonetheless is the clue to the form of Proust's vast structure.

Every reader soon notices that Proust does not follow any of his characters continuously through the whole course of his novel, Instead, they appear and reappear in various stages of their lives. Hundreds of pages sometimes go by between the time they are last seen and the time they reappear; and when they do turn up again, the passage of time has invariably changed them in some decisive way. Rather than being submerged in the stream of time and intuiting a character progressively, in a continuous line of development, the reader is confronted with various snapshots of the characters "motionless in a moment of vision" taken at different stages in their lives; and in juxtaposing these images he experiences the effects of the passage of time exactly as the narrator had done. As Proust has promised, therefore, he does stamp his novel indelibly with the form of time; but we are now in a position to understand exactly what he meant by this engagement.

To experience the passage of time, Proust had learned, it was necessary to rise above it and to grasp both past and present simultaneously in a moment of what he called "pure time." But "pure time," obviously, is not time at all—it is perception in a moment of time, that is to say, space. And, by the discontinuous presentation of character Proust forces the reader to juxtapose disparate images spatially, in a moment of time, so that the experience of time's passage is communicated directly to his sensibility. Ramon Fernandez has acutely stressed this point in some remarks on Proust and Bergson. "Much attention has been given to the importance of time in Proust's work," he writes, "but perhaps it has not been sufficiently noted that he gives time the value and characteristics of space . . . in affirming that the different parts of time reciprocally exclude and remain external to each other." And he adds that, while Proust's method of making contact with his *durée* is quite Bergsonian (that is, springing from the interpenetration of the past with the present), "the reactions of his intelligence on his sensibility, which determine the trajectory of his work, would orient him rather toward a *spatialisation* of time and memory." [10]

There is a striking analogy here between Proust's method and that of his beloved Impressionist painters; but this analogy goes far deeper than the usual comments about the "impressionism" of Proust's style. The Impressionist painters juxtaposed pure tones on the canvas, instead of mixing them on the palette, in order to leave the blending of colors to the eye of the spectator. Similarly, Proust gives us what might be called pure views of his characters—views of them "motionless in a moment of vision" in various phases of their lives—and allows the sensibility of the reader to fuse these views into a unity. Each view must be apprehended by the reader as a unit; and Proust's purpose is achieved only when these units of meaning are referred to each other reflexively in a moment of time. As with Joyce and the modern poets, spatial form is also the structural scaffolding of Proust's labyrinthine masterpiece.

V. *Djuna Barnes:* Nightwood

The name of Djuna Barnes first became known to those readers who followed, with any care, the stream of pamphlets, books, magazines, and anthologies that poured forth to enlighten America in the feverish days of literary expatriation. Miss Barnes, it is true, must always have remained a somewhat enigmatic figure even to the most attentive reader. Born in New York State, she spent most of her time in England and France; and the glimpses one catches of her in the memoirs of the period are brief and unrevealing. She appears in *The Dial* from time to time with a drawing or a poem; she crops up now and again in some anthology of avant-garde writers—the usual agglomeration of people who are later to become famous or to sink into the melancholy oblivion of frustrated promise. Before the publication of *Nightwood*, indeed, one might have been inclined to place her name in the latter group. For while she had a book of short stories and an earlier novel to her credit, neither prepares one for the maturity of achievement so conspicuous in every line of this work.[11]

Of the fantastical quality of her imagination, of the gift for imagery that, as T. S. Eliot has said in his preface to *Nightwood*, gives one a sense of horror and doom akin to Elizabethan tragedy, of the epigrammatic incisiveness of her phrasing and her penchant, also akin to the Elizabethans, for dealing with the more scabrous manifestations of human fallibility—of all these there is evidence in *Ryder*, Miss Barnes's first novel. But all this might well have resulted only in a momentary flare-up of capri-

cious brilliance, whose radiance would have been as
dazzling as it was insubstantial. *Ryder*, it must be con-
fessed, is an anomalous creation from any point of view.
Although Miss Barnes's unusual qualities gradually
emerge from its kaleidoscope of moods and styles, these
qualities are still, so to speak, held in solution or at best
placed in the service of a literary *jeu d'esprit*. Only in
Nightwood do they finally crystallize into a definitive and
comprehensible pattern.

Many critics—not least among them T. S. Eliot—have
paid tribute to *Nightwood*'s compelling intensity, its head-
and-shoulders superiority, simply as a stylistic phenomenon, to most of the works that currently pass for literature. But *Nightwood*'s reputation is similar, in many
respects, to that of *The Waste Land* in 1922—it is known
as a collection of striking passages, some of breathtak-
ing poetic quality, appealing chiefly to connoisseurs of
somewhat gamy literary items. Such a reputation, it
need hardly be remarked, is not conducive to intelligent
appreciation or understanding. Thanks to a good many
critics, we have become able to approach *The Waste Land*
as a work of art rather than as a battleground for opposing poetic theories or as a curious piece of literary eso-
terica. It is time that we began to approach *Nightwood* in
the same way.

Before dealing with *Nightwood* in detail, however, we
must make certain broad distinctions between it and the
novels already considered. While the structural principle of *Nightwood* is the same as of *Ulysses* and *A la recherche du temps perdu*—spatial form, obtained by means
of reflexive reference—there are marked differences in
technique that will be obvious to every reader. Taking
an analogy from another art, we can say that these differences are similar to those between the work of Cézanne
and the compositions of a later and more abstract painter

like Braque. What characterizes the work of Cézanne, above all, is the tension between two conflicting but deeply rooted tendencies. On the one hand, there is the struggle to attain aesthetic form—conceived of by Cézanne as a self-enclosed unity of form-and-color harmonies—and, on the other, the desire to create this form through the recognizable depiction of natural objects. Later artists took over only Cézanne's preoccupation with formal harmonies, omitting natural objects altogether or presenting them in some distorted manner.

Like Cézanne, Proust and Joyce accept the naturalistic principle, presenting their characters in terms of those commonplace details, those descriptions of circumstance and environment, that we have come to regard as verisimilar. Their experiments with the novel form, it is true, were inspired by a desire to conform more closely to the experience of consciousness; but while the principle of verisimilitude was shifted from the external to the internal, it was far from being abandoned. At the same time, these writers intended to control the abundance of verisimilar detail reflected through consciousness by the unity of spatial apprehension. But in *Nightwood*, as in the work of Braque, the Fauves or the Cubists, the naturalistic principle has lost its dominance. We are asked only to accept the work of art as an autonomous structure giving us an individual vision of reality; and the question of the relation of this vision to an extra-artistic "objective" world has ceased to have any fundamental importance.

To illustrate the transition that takes place in *Nightwood*, we may examine an interesting passage from Proust where the process can be caught at a rudimentary level. In describing Robert de Saint-Loup, an important character in the early sections of the novel, the narrator tells us that he could see concealed "beneath a courtier's smile his warrior's thirst for action—when I examined him I could see how closely the vigorous structure of his triangular face must have been modelled on that of his ancestors' faces, a face devised rather for an ardent bowman than for a delicate student. Beneath his fine skin the bold construction, the feudal architecture, were apparent. His head made one think of those old dungeon keeps on which the disused battlements are still to be seen, although inside they have been converted into libraries."

By the time the reader comes across this passage he has already learned a considerable number of facts about Saint-Loup. The latter, he knows, is a member of the Guermantes family, one of the oldest and most aristocratic in the French nobility and still the acknowledged leaders of Parisian society. Unlike their feudal ancestors, however, the Guermantes have no real influence over the internal affairs of France under the Third Republic. Moreover, Saint-Loup is by way of being a family black sheep. Seemingly uninterested in social success, a devoted student of Nietzsche and Proudhon, he was "imbued with the most profound contempt for his caste." Knowing these facts from earlier sections of the novel, the reader accepts the passage quoted above simply as a trenchant summation of Saint-Loup's character. But so precisely do the images in this passage apply to everything the reader has learned about Saint-Loup, so exactly do they communicate the central impression of his personality, that it would be possible to derive a total knowledge of his character solely from the images without attaching them to a set of external social and historical details.

Images of this kind are commoner in poetry than in prose—more particularly, since we are speaking of character description, in dramatic poetry. In Shakespeare

and the Elizabethans, descriptions of characters are not
"realistic" as we understand the word today. They are
not a collection of circumstantial details whose bare
conglomeration is assumed to convey a personality. The
dramatic poet, rather, defined both physical and psychological aspects of character at one stroke, in an image
or a series of images. Here is Antony, for example, as
Shakespeare presents him in the opening scene of *Antony and Cleopatra:*

> Nay, but this dotage of our general's
> O'erflows the measure: those his goodly eyes
> That o'er the files and musters of the war
> Have glow'd like plated Mars, now bend, now turn,
> The office and devotion of their view
> Upon a tawny front: his captain's heart,
> Which in the scuffles of great fights hath burst
> The buckles on his breast, reneges all temper,
> And is become the bellows and the fan
> To cool a gipsy's lust.

And then, to complete the picture, Antony is contemptuously called the "triple pillar of the world transform'd
into a strumpet's fool."

Or, to take a more modern example, from a poet (T. S.
Eliot) strongly influenced by the Elizabethans, here is
the twentieth-century Everyman:

> He, the young man carbuncular, arrives,
> A small house agent's clerk, with one bold stare,
> One of the low on whom assurance sits
> As a silk hat on a Bradford millionaire.

As Ramon Fernandez has remarked of similar character
descriptions in the work of George Meredith, images of

this kind analyze without dissociating. They describe character but at the same time hold fast to the unity of personality, without splintering it to fragments in trying to seize the secret of its integration.[12]

Writing of this order—charged with symbolic overtones—pierces through the cumbrous mass of naturalistic detail to express the essence of character in an image; it is the antithesis to the reigning convention in the novel. Ordinary novels, as T. S. Eliot justly observes, "obtain what reality they have largely from an accurate rendering of the noises that human beings currently make in their daily simple needs of communication; and what part of a novel is not composed of these noises consists of a prose which is no more alive than that of a competent newspaper writer or government official." Miss Barnes abandons any pretensions to this kind of verisimilitude, just as modern painters have abandoned any attempt at naturalistic representation; and the result is a world as strange to the reader, at first sight, as the world of Cubism was to its first spectators. Since the selection of detail in *Nightwood* is governed not by the logic of verisimilitude but by the demands of the décor necessary to enhance the symbolic significance of the characters, the novel has baffled even its most fascinated admirers. Let us attack the mystery by applying our method of reflexive reference, instead of approaching the book, as most of its readers have done, in terms of a coherent temporal pattern of narrative.

Since *Nightwood* lacks a narrative structure in the ordinary sense, it cannot be reduced to any sequence of action for purposes of explanation. One can, if one chooses, follow the narrator in Proust through the various stages of his social career; one can, with some difficulty, follow Leopold Bloom's epic journey through

Dublin; but no such reduction is possible in *Nightwood*. As Dr. O'Connor remarks to Nora Flood, with his desperate gaiety: "I have a narrative, but you will be put to it to find it." Strictly speaking, the doctor is wrong—he has a static situation, not a narrative, and no matter how hard the reader looks he will find only the various facets of this situation explored from different angles. The eight chapters of *Nightwood* are like searchlights, probing the darkness each from a different direction yet ultimately illuminating the same entanglement of the human spirit.

In the first four chapters we are introduced to each of the important persons—Felix Volkbein, Nora Flood, Robin Vote, Jenny Petherbridge, and Dr. O'Connor. The next three chapters are, for the most part, long monologues by the doctor, through which the developments of the earlier chapters begin to take on meaning. The last chapter, only a few pages long, has the effect of a coda, giving us what we have already come to feel is the only possible termination. And these chapters are knit together, not by the progress of any action—either narrative action or, as in a stream-of-consciousness novel, the flow of experience—but by the continual reference and cross reference of images and symbols that must be referred to each other spatially throughout the time-act of reading.

At first sight, Dr. O'Connor's brilliant and fantastic monologues seem to dominate the book and overshadow the other characters; but the central figure—the figure around which the situation revolves—is in reality Robin Vote. This creation—it is impossible to call her a character, since character implies humanity and she has not yet attained the level of the human—is one of the most remarkable figures in contemporary literature. We meet her first when the doctor, sitting and drinking with Felix Volkbein in a Paris bar, is summoned by a bellboy from a nearby hotel to look after a lady who has fainted and cannot be awakened. "The perfume that her body exhaled," Miss Barnes writes of Robin,

was of the quality of that earth-flesh, fungi, which smells of captured dampness and yet is so dry, overcast with the odor of oil of amber, which is an inner malady of the sea, making her seem as if she had invaded a sleep incautious and entire. Her flesh was the texture of plant life, and beneath it one sensed a frame, broad, porous and sleep-worn, as if sleep were a decay fishing her beneath the visible surface. About her head there was an effulgence as of phosphorus growing about the circumference of a body of water— as if her life lay through her in ungainly luminous deteriorations—the troubling structure of the born somnambule, who lives in two worlds—meet of child and desperado.

Taken by itself, this description is likely to prove more confusing than enlightening; but a few pages later another attempt is made to explain Robin's significance:

Sometimes one meets a woman who is beast turning human. Such a person's every movement will reduce to an image of a forgotten experience; a mirage of an eternal wedding cast on the racial memory; as insupportable a joy as would be the vision of an eland coming down an aisle of trees, chapleted with orange blossoms and bridal veil, a hoof raised in the economy of fear, stepping in the trepidation of flesh that will become a myth.

It is significant that we first meet Robin—*la somnambule*, the sleepwalker—when she is being awakened; before that moment we have no knowledge of her life. Her life might be said to begin with that moment, and the act of awakening to be the act of birth.

From these descriptions we begin to realize that Robin symbolizes a state of existence which is before, rather than beyond, good and evil. She is both innocent and depraved—meet of child and desperado—precisely because she has not reached the human state where moral values become relevant. Lacking responsibility of any kind, abandoning herself to wayward and perverse passions, she yet has the innocence and purity of a child. (Nora tells the doctor in the seventh chapter that Robin played "with her toys, trains, and animals and cars to wind up, and dolls and marbles and toy soldiers.") Gliding through life like a sleepwalker, living in a dream from which she has not awakened—Robin is at once completely egotistical and yet lacking in a sense of her own identity.

"And why does Robin feel innocent?" Dr. O'Connor asks, when Nora, Robin's lover, comes to him with her agonizing questions. "Every bed she leaves, without caring, fills her heart with peace and happiness. . . . She knows she is innocent because she can't do anything in relation to anyone but herself." But at the same time the doctor tells Felix, Robin's erstwhile husband, that Robin had written from America saying, "Remember me." "Probably," he remarks, "because she has difficulty in remembering herself." By taking these passages together, we can understand what the doctor means when he says that "Robin was outside the 'human type'—a wild thing caught in a woman's skin, monstrously alone, monstrously vain."

The situation of the novel, then, revolves around this extraordinary creature. Robin, Felix eagerly confides to the doctor, "always seemed to be looking for someone to tell her that she was innocent. . . . There are some people who must get permission to live, and if the Baronin [Robin] finds no one to give her that permission, she will make an innocence for herself; a fearful sort of primitive innocence." To be conscious of one's innocence, of course, implies a consciousness of moral value that, we have seen, Robin does not possess. If Robin could have found someone to tell her that she was innocent, she would have found someone who had raised her to the level of the human—someone who had given her "permission to live" as a human being, not merely to exist as an amorphous mass of moral possibility.

Once this fundamental problem is grasped, much of what we read in the rest of *Nightwood* becomes considerably clearer. At the beginning of the book we are introduced to Felix Volkbein, a Viennese half-Jew with a somewhat questionable title. What Miss Barnes says of Felix immediately gives him the same type of symbolic stature that Robin possesses:

> What had formed Felix from the date of his birth to his coming to thirty was unknown to the world, for the step of the wandering Jew is in every son. No matter where and when you meet him you feel that he has come from . . . some secret land that he has been nourished on but cannot inherit, for the Jew seems to be everywhere from nowhere. When Felix's name was mentioned, three or more persons would swear to having seen him the week before in three different countries simultaneously.

Combined with this aspect of Felix is a curious "obsession for what he termed 'Old Europe': aristocracy, nobility, royalty. . . . He felt that the great past might mend a little if he bowed low enough, if he succumbed and gave homage." Immediately after seeing Robin, Felix confesses to the doctor that he "wished a son who would feel as he felt about the 'great past.'" "To pay homage to our past," he says, "is the only gesture that also includes the future." He pays court to Robin and, since her "life held no volition for refusal," they marry. Felix, then, makes the first effort to shape Robin, to give her permission to live by informing her with his own sense of moral values. He does so because he senses, almost instinctively, that with Robin "anything can be done."

Felix fails with Robin, just as do the others who try to provide her with a moral framework. But what exactly does Felix's failure imply? In other words, what is the sense of values that proves inadequate to lifting Robin to the level of the human? Because Felix is so astonishingly individual a creation, despite the broader significance of his role in the novel, this is a particularly difficult question to answer. Some clue may be found if we remind ourselves of another Wandering Jew in modern fiction, Leopold Bloom. Seeking for a character to typify *l'homme moyen sensuel*, not only of our own time but through all history, Joyce chose the figure of a Wandering Jew vainly trying to integrate himself into a culture to which he is essentially alien. And this predicament of the Jew is merely a magnification of the predicament of modern man himself, bewildered and homeless in a mechanical wilderness of his own creation. If Felix is viewed in this light, we may understand his dubious title, his abject reverence for the great tradition of the past, and his frantic desire to assimilate this tradition to himself, as so many examples of a basic need to feel at home in some cultural framework.

Until his meeting with Robin, Felix's relationship to what he considered the great traditions of the European past had been completely negative. The first chapter of the novel, dominated by Felix, is appropriately entitled "Bow Down"—for this phrase defines Felix's attitude toward the great tradition, even toward its trivial and unworthy modern representatives. "In restaurants he bowed slightly to anyone who looked as if he might be 'someone,' making the bow so imperceptible that the surprised person might think he was merely adjusting his stomach." The doctor links this blind, unthinking worship of the aristocratic traditions of the past with the attitude of the masses in general toward an aristocracy they have falsely deified; and he lights up in a flash the symbolic meaning of Felix's obsession.

"Nobility, very well, but what is it?" The Baron started to answer him, but the doctor held up his hand. "Wait a minute! I know—the few that the many have lied about well and long enough to make them deathless." Felix is in the position of the masses, the common men, desperately lying to themselves about an inherited sense of values which they know only by its external trappings. But by marrying Robin, the doctor realizes, Felix is staking his existence on the belief that these traditional values still have vitality—that they will succeed in shaping the primeval chaos of Robin into order. (On Felix's first visit to court Robin he carries two volumes on the life of the Bourbons.) Knowing that Felix's attempt is doomed to failure, the doctor makes an effort to warn him: "The last muscle of aristocracy is madness—remember that" —the doctor leaned forward—"the last child born to aristocracy is sometimes an idiot. . . . So I say beware! In the king's bed is always found, just before it becomes a museum piece, the droppings of the black sheep."

Robin does bear Felix a sickly, stunted, prematurely aged, possibly feebleminded child—the droppings of the black sheep. And, after unwillingly conceiving the child "amid loud and frantic cries of affirmation and despair," Robin leaves Felix. The child had meant for Felix the creative reaffirmation of the great European aristocratic tradition; but Robin's flight reveals that this tradition is impotent. It contains nothing for the future except the wistful and precocious senility of Guido, Felix's child.

The next character to enter the lists with Robin is Nora Flood, who comes perhaps closest of all to giving Robin "permission to live." Nora, as a symbolic figure, is given meaning on a number of levels; but the title of the third chapter, "Night Watch," expresses the essence of her spiritual attitude. We are told that she keeps "a 'paupers' salon for poets, radicals, beggars, artists, and people in love; for Catholics, Protestants, Brahmins, dabblers in black magic and medicine"—this last, of course, being an allusion to the doctor. Nora was "by temperament an early Christian; she believed the word"; this meant that she "robbed herself for everyone. . . . Wandering people the world over found her profitable in that she could be sold for a price forever, for she carried her betrayal money in her own pocket."

It is significant that Nora is described in images of the American West: "Looking at her, foreigners remembered stories they had heard of covered wagons; animals going down to drink; children's heads, just as far as the eyes, looking in fright out of small windows, where in the dark another race crouched in ambush." These images, Nora's paupers' salon, and her early Christian temperament all represent different crystallizations of the same spiritual attitude. Among the determinants of this attitude are a belief in the innate goodness of man (or at least in his capacity for moral improvement), a belief in progress, and an indiscriminate approbation of all forms of ethical and intellectual unconventionality—in short, the complete antithesis to the world of values represented by Felix. Irving Babbitt would have called Nora a hopeless Rousseauist, and he would have been right.

Characteristically, while Felix was drawn to Robin because he wished to use her, Nora is drawn to her through pity. The scene in which Nora meets Robin is important not only for what it reveals of their relationship, but also because there is a passage that confirms our interpretation of Robin. Both Robin and Nora are watching a circus performance when,

> As one powerful lioness came to the turn of the bars, exactly opposite the girl [Robin], she turned her furious great head with its yellow eyes afire and went down, her paws thrust through the bars and, as she regarded the girl, as if a river were falling behind impassable heat, her eyes flowed in tears that never reached the surface.

Being neither animal nor human, Robin evokes pity from both species. Nora, intuitively understanding Robin's perturbation at the lioness's stare, takes her by the hand and leads her outside. And, although strangers until that moment, Robin is soon telling Nora "her wish for a home, as if she were afraid she would be lost again, as if she were aware, without conscious knowledge, that she belonged to Nora, and that if Nora did not make it permanent by her own strength, she would forget." What Robin would forget was where she belonged, her own identity, given to her at least for a while by the strength of Nora's love and pity.

Nora's failure with Robin is already foreshadowed in the first description of Nora as having "the face of all people who love the people—a face that would be evil when she found out that to love without criticism is to be betrayed." While Felix had deliberately tried to shape Robin, Nora simply envelops her in an all-embracing love that, because of Nora's belief in natural goodness, has no room for praise or blame. "In court," we read, Nora "would have been impossible; no one would have been hanged, reproached or forgiven because no one would have been accused." With a creature like Robin, the result was inevitable. Nora's self-sacrificing devotion does succeed for a time in giving Robin a sense of identity. Robin's unconditional acceptance by Nora, exactly as she is, eases the tension between the animal and the human that is tearing Robin's life apart; but in the end Nora is not able to give Robin "permission to live" any more than Felix could. Most of the third chapter of the novel is given over to an analysis of this slow estrangement between Robin and Nora, an estrangement all the more torturous because, while desired by neither, it is recognized as inevitable by both.

Yet the quality of Robin's relationship with Nora shows how much more closely Nora came to success than Felix. With Felix Robin had been passive, almost disinterested, in conformity with her somnambulistic nature. Although her life was a frenzy of activity, she never really acted in more than an animal sense; Robin's acts were always reactions to obscure impulses whose meaning she did not understand. With Nora, however, there are moments when Robin realizes the terror of their inevitable separation; and in these moments, clinging to

Nora like a child, Robin becomes almost human because her terror reveals an implicit moral choice.

Yet sometimes, going about the house, in passing each other, they would fall into an agonized embrace, looking into each other's face, their two heads in their four hands, so strained together that the space that divided them seemed to be thrusting them apart. Sometimes in these moments of insurmountable grief Robin would make some movement, use a peculiar turn of phrase not habitual to her, innocent of the betrayal, by which Nora was informed that Robin had come from a world to which she would return. To keep her (in Robin there was this tragic longing to be kept, knowing herself astray) Nora knew now that there was no way but death.

As usual, the appropriate comment on this situation is made by the doctor, seeing Nora out roaming the streets at night in search of Robin. "'There goes the dismantled—Love has fallen off her wall. A religious woman,' he thought to himself, 'without the joy and safety of the Catholic faith, which at a pinch covers up the spots on the wall when the family portraits take a slide; take that safety from a woman,' he said to himself, quickening his steps to follow her, 'and love gets loose and into the rafters. She sees her everywhere,' he added, glancing at Nora as she passed into the dark. 'Out looking for what she's afraid to find—Robin. There goes the mother of mischief, running about, trying to get the world home.'" Robin, it should be noticed, is identified with "the world"—which may mean that the world is really no better off than she is—and Nora's failure with Robin, or rather her derangement over this failure, is attributed to her lack of the Catholic faith.

The doctor does not say that the Catholic faith would have allowed Nora to control Robin by giving her a framework of moral values, but he does say that, if Nora had been a Catholic, the eccentricities of Robin's nature would not have plunged her into an abyss of self-torture and suffering. It is Nora's faith in natural goodness, her uncritical acceptance of Robin because of this faith, that has caused her to suffer. The doctor implies that as a Catholic she would have been able to rationalize Robin's nature in terms of the Catholic understanding of sin and evil; and while this would not have prevented the evil, it would certainly have eased the disillusionment and suffering. As we shall see later, this passage is crucial to an understanding of the book as a whole.

Nora realizes that Robin is lost to her when, at dawn, she looks out the window and sees another woman "her arms about Robin's neck, her body pressed to Robin's, her legs slackened in the hang of the embrace." This other woman, Jenny Petherbridge, is the only person in the novel without a trace of tragic grandeur—and this is not surprising, for she is depicted as the essence of mediocrity, the incarnation of the second-hand and the second-rate.

Chapter four, in which she makes her main appearance, is appropriately entitled "The Squatter." For her life is a continual infringement on the rights of other people, an infringement that becomes permanent merely by the power of persistence. "Her walls, her cupboards, her bureaux, were teeming with second-hand dealings with life. It takes a bold and authentic robber to get first-hand plunder. Someone else's marriage ring was on her finger; the photograph taken of Robin for Nora sat upon her table."

Jenny, again, is the only person in the novel who

might be called bourgeois; and there is more than a touch of the *nouveau riche* in her ostentation and her lavishness with money. Wanting to possess anything that had importance, "she appropriated the most passionate love that she knew, Nora's for Robin." Jenny's relationship to Robin differs from those of Felix and Nora, for she has no intuition of Robin's pathetic moral emptiness; nor does she seize on Robin as a teeming chaos of vitality through which to realize her own values. She simply appropriates Robin as another acquisition to her collection of objects that other people have valued. Staking her claim to Robin immediately after Nora, Jenny's main function in the novel seems that of underlining the hopelessness of Robin's plight. To fall from Nora to Jenny—to exchange the moral world of one for the moral world of the other—is only too convincing a proof that Robin has still failed to acquire any standards of value.

At the conclusion of the fourth chapter, when we learn that Robin and Jenny have sailed for America, the novel definitely shifts its focus. Until this point Robin has been its center both spiritually and actually; but Robin now drops out of sight—though she is talked about at great length—and does not appear directly again until the brief concluding episode.

The next three chapters are completely dominated by the doctor. "Dr. Matthew-Mighty-grain-of-salt-Dante-O'Connor," whose dialogues with Felix and Nora—or rather his monologues, prompted by their questions—make up the bulk of these pages. The doctor serves as commentator on the events of the novel, if events they can be called; and as T. S. Eliot says of Tiresias in *The Waste Land*, what he sees, in fact, is the substance of the novel.

This comparison can bear closer application. There is

an evident—and probably not accidental—similarity between the two figures. Like the man-woman Tiresias, symbol of universal experience, the doctor has homosexual inclinations; like Tiresias he has "fore-suffered all" by apparently being immortal (he claims to have a "prehistoric memory," and is always talking as if he had existed in other historical periods). Like Tiresias again, who "walked among the lowest of the dead," the doctor is father confessor to the creatures of the night world who inhabit the novel as well as being an inhabitant of that world himself. And in his role of commentator, the doctor "perceived the scene, and foretold the rest." For these reasons, Nora comes to him with the burning question—the title of the fifth chapter—"Watchman, What of the Night?"

It is impossible to give any exact idea of the doctor's monologues except by quoting them at length; and that would unduly prolong an already protracted analysis. But to find anything approaching their combination of ironic wit and religious humility, their emotional subtlety and profound human simplicity, their pathos, their terror, and their sophisticated self-consciousness, one has to go back to the religious sonnets of John Donne. It is these monologues that prove the main attraction of the novel at first reading, and their magnetic power has, no doubt, contributed to the misconception that *Nightwood* is only a collection of magnificent fragments. Moreover, since the doctor always speaks about himself *sub specie aeternitatis*, it is difficult at first to grasp the relations between his monologues and the central theme of the novel.

T. S. Eliot notes in his preface that he could place the doctor in proper focus only after a number of readings;

and this is likely to be the experience of other readers as well. But as Eliot rightly emphasizes, the book cannot be understood unless the doctor is seen as part of the whole pattern, rather than as an overwhelming individual creation who throws the others into the background by the magnitude of his understanding and the depth of his insight. Now that the pattern has been sketched, we can safely approach the doctor a little more closely and explain his individual spiritual attitude. It is this attitude that, in the end, dominates the book and gives it a final focus.

"Man," the doctor tells Felix, "was born damned and innocent from the start, and wretchedly—as he must—on those two themes—whistles his tune." Robin, it will be remembered, was described as both child and desperado, that is, both damned and innocent; and since the doctor generalizes her spiritual predicament, we can infer that he views the condition of the other characters—and of himself—as in essentials no different. The doctor, who calls himself "the god of darkness," is a good illustration of his own statement. He is damned by his excess of the knowledge of evil, which condemns him to a living death. "You know what none of us know until we have died," Nora tells him. "You were dead in the beginning." But beyond the doctor's knowledge, beyond his twisted bitterness, is the pathos of abused innocence. "No matter what I may be doing," he cries, "in my heart is the wish for children and knitting. God, I never asked better than to boil some good man's potatoes and toss up a child for him every nine months by the calendar." And after the striking Tiny O'Toole episode, in which the doctor reveals all his saintlike simplicity (his attitude toward animals is reminiscent of St.

Francis of Assisi) Nora says: "Sometimes I don't know
why I talk to you. You're so like a child; then again I
know well enough."

Because of his knowledge of man's nature, the doctor
realizes that he himself, and the other people in the
novel, differ from Robin only in degree; they are all involved to some extent in her desperate dualism, and in
the end their doom is equally inescapable. "We are but
skin about a wind," he says, "with muscles clenched
against mortality. . . . Life, the permission to know
death." Come to ask the "god of darkness" about that
fabulous night-creature Robin, Nora draws the only
possible conclusion from the doctor's harangues: "I'll
never understand her—I'll always be miserable—just
like this?" To which the doctor responds by one of his
tirades that seems to be about nothing in particular, and
yet turns out to be about everything.

The essential quality in the doctor that grows upon
the reader is the practical futility of his knowledge, his
own hopelessness and helplessness. In the early chapters he turns up occasionally, exhibiting an insight into
the other people that they themselves do not possess
and seeming to stand outside their dilemmas. But as the
doctor comes to the foreground, we find this impression
completely erroneous. He talks because he knows there
is nothing else to do—and because to stop talking would
be to think, and to think would be unbearable.

> "Look here," said the doctor. "Do you know what has
> made me the greatest liar this side of the moon, telling
> my stories to people like you to take the mortal agony
> out of their guts . . . to stop them from . . . staring
> over their knuckles with misery which they are trying

to keep off, saying, 'Say something, Doctor, for the love of God!' And me talking away like mad. Well, that, and nothing else, has made me the liar I am."

And in another place he sums it up succinctly: "I talk too much because I have been made so miserable by what you're keeping hushed."

Still, the doctor cannot always maintain this role; he cannot always drown his own agony in a flood of talk for the benefit of others. And so, his own tension exacerbated by Nora's increasing hysteria, he bursts forth:

"Do you think, for Christ's sweet sake, that I am so happy that you should cry down my neck? Do you think there is no lament in this world, but your own? . . . A broken heart have you! [he says scornfully, a few sentences later] "I have falling arches, flying dandruff, a floating kidney, shattered nerves and a broken heart! . . . Am I going forward screaming that it hurts . . . or holding my guts as if they were a coil of knives? . . . Do I wail to the mountains of the trouble I have had in the valley, or to every stone of the way it broke my bones, or of every life, how it went down into my belly and built a nest to hatch me my death there?"

It is on this note that we take leave of the doctor, cursing "the people in my life who have made my life miserable, coming to me to learn of degradation and the night."

But, although the doctor as an individual ends on a note of complete negation, this is not his final judgment on the total pattern of the novel—it is only his final verdict on himself. His attitude toward Robin and the people surrounding her is somewhat more complex. We have already indicated the nature of this complexity by quoting the doctor's remark, when he sees Nora wandering through the streets in search of Robin, that she was a religious woman "without the joy and safety of the Catholic faith, which at a pinch covers up the spots on the wall when the family portraits take a slide." There may be nothing to do about Robin's situation—man's attempts to achieve a truly human existence have always ended in failure; but there is at least the consolation of what the doctor calls "the girl that you love so much that she can lie to you"—the Catholic Church. Discussing the confessional with Felix, the doctor describes it as the place where, although a person may lack genuine contrition, "mischief unravels and the fine high hand of Heaven proffers the skein again, combed and forgiven."

It would be unwise to bear down too heavily on this point and make the doctor's attitude more positive than it actually is. His Catholicism, although deeply rooted in his emotional nature, can offer consolation but not hope; and even its consolation is a puny thing compared to the realities of the human situation as the doctor knows it. "I, as good a Catholic as they make," he tells Nora, "have embraced every confection of hope, and yet I know well, for all our outcry and struggle, we shall be for the next generation not the massive dung fallen from the dinosaur, but the little speck left of the humming-bird."

If the doctor derives any consolation from his Catholicism, it is the consolation of Pascal contemplating the wretchedness and insignificance of man rather than that of Thomas Aquinas admiring an orderly and rational moral universe. "Be humble like the dust, as God intended, and crawl," he advises Nora, "and finally you'll crawl to the end of the gutter and not be missed and not much remembered." What the doctor would like to attain is the spiritual attitude that T. S. Eliot prays for in *Ash Wednesday:*

> Teach us to care and not to care
> Teach us to sit still.

The doctor cannot reach this state because he is too deeply involved in the sufferings of others ("I was doing well enough," he says to Nora, "until you came and kicked my stone over, and out I came, all moss and eyes"), but he recognizes it as the only attitude offering some measure of inner peace.

Since the doctor is not the center of the pattern in *Nightwood,* the novel cannot end merely with his last appearance. We know Robin's fate from his monologues, but we have not had it presented to us dramatically; all we know is that Robin has gone to America with Jenny. The brief last chapter fills this gap and furnishes, with the inevitability of great tragedy, the only possible conclusion.

Robin soon leaves Jenny in America and, impelled by some animal instinct, makes her way to where Nora lives. Without Nora's knowledge she lives in the woods of Nora's estate—we are not told how, and it is of no importance—sleeping in a decaying chapel belonging to Nora's family. One night Nora's watchdog scents Robin, and Nora, hearing the dog bark, follows him to investigate. Entering the chapel, she is witness to this strange and horrible scene between Robin and the dog:

> Sliding down she [Robin] went . . . until her head
> swung against his [the dog's]; on all fours now, drag-

ging her knees. The veins stood out in her neck, swelled in her arms, and wide and throbbing rose up on her fingers as she moved forward. . . . Then she began to bark also, crawling after him—barking in a fit of laughter, obscene and touching. The dog began to cry then . . . and she grinning and crying with him; crying in shorter and shorter spaces, moving head to head, until she gave up, lying out, her hands beside her, her face turned and weeping; and the dog too gave up then, his eyes bloodshot, his head flat along her knees.

What this indicates, clearly, is that Robin has abandoned her efforts to rise to the human and is returning to the animal state; the somnambule is entering her age-old sleep.

So ends this amazing book, which combines the simple majesty of a medieval morality play with the verbal subtlety and refinement of a Symbolist poem. This exposition, of course, has barely skimmed its surface; there are ramifications of the various characters that need a detailed exegesis far beyond the scope of my intention. But, limited as it is, the discussion should have proved one point. *Nightwood* does have a pattern—a pattern arising from the spatial interweaving of images and phrases independently of any time-sequence of narrative action. And, as in *The Waste Land*, the reader is simply bewildered if he assumes that, because language proceeds in time, *Nightwood* must be perceived as a narrative structure. We can now understand why T. S. Eliot wrote that "*Nightwood* will appeal primarily to readers of poetry," and that "it is so good a novel that only sensibilities trained on poetry can wholly appreciate it." Since the unit of meaning in *Nightwood* is usually a phrase or sequence of phrases—at most a long paragraph—it carries the evolution of spatial form in the novel forward to a point where it is practically indistinguishable from modern poetry.

VI. The Parallel with the Plastic Arts

All the works so far considered are thus structurally similar in their employment of spatial form. And the question naturally arises of how to account for this surprising unanimity. But to answer this question satisfactorily, we must first widen the bounds of our analysis and consider the more general problem of the relation of art forms to the cultural climates in which they are created. This latter issue has attracted the attention of students of the arts at least since the time of Herder and Winckelmann; and Hegel, in his *Vorlesungen über die Aesthetik*, gave a masterly analysis of various art styles as sensuous objectifications of diverse *Weltanschauungen*.

Stimulated by this intellectual heritage, and by the vast increase in historical knowledge accumulated during the nineteenth century, a group of German and Austrian art scholars and critics concentrated on the problem of form in the plastic arts. In a series of works published during the first quarter of the present century, they defined various categories of form in the plastic arts, traced in detail the shift from one form to another, and attempted to account for these changes of form by changes in the general cultural ambience.[13] T. E. Hulme, one of the few writers in English to have seriously concerned himself with the problem of form in literature, turned to this group for guidance; and we can do no better than to follow his example.

One German writer in particular exercised a strong influence on Hulme and through Hulme, by way of

Eliot, probably on the whole of modern English criticism. This writer is Wilhelm Worringer, the author of the important book, *Abstraction and Empathy* (subtitled *A Contribution to the Psychology of Style*);[14] and it is in Worringer that we shall find the key to the problem of spatial form. Worringer's book appeared in 1908 as its author's doctoral dissertation, but despite this academic provenance it quickly went through numerous editions.

This fact proves—as Worringer himself notes in his third edition—that his subject was not merely academic but touched on problems vital to the modern sensibility. Moreover, as Worringer further remarks, while he and other scholars were rescuing and reevaluating neglected nonnaturalistic styles, creative artists at the very same moment were turning to these styles for inspiration. Worringer's book is impeccably scholastic, confining itself strictly to the past and excluding all but the briefest references to the art of his contemporaries; but it is nonetheless of the utmost relevance for modern art. And this relevance, along with Worringer's unusually expressive and incisive style, gives the book its noticeable quality of intellectual excitement and discovery—a quality that it retains even at the present time, when most of its ideas have become part of the standard jargon of art criticism.

The problem that Worringer sets out to solve is why, throughout the history of the plastic arts, there has been a continual alternation between naturalistic and nonnaturalistic styles. Periods of naturalism have included the classical age of Greek art, the Italian Renaissance, and the art of Western Europe to the end of the nineteenth century. In these eras the artist strives to represent the objective, three-dimensional world of "natural" vision and to reproduce with loving accuracy the processes and forms of organic nature (among which man is included). Periods of nonnaturalism include most of primitive art, Egyptian monumental sculpture, Byzantine art, Romanesque sculpture, the dominant art styles of the twentieth century. In these eras the artist abandons the projection of space entirely and returns to the plane, reduces organic nature to linear-geometric forms, and frequently eliminates all traces of organicism in favor of pure lines, forms, and colors. To be sure, there are vast differences between the styles of various periods thrown together in these rough categories; but the basic similarities between the works in one category and their basic opposition, taken as a group, to all the styles in the other category are no less striking and instructive. Worringer argues that we have here a fundamental polarity between two distinct types of creation in the plastic arts. And, most important of all, neither can be set up as the norm to which the other must adhere.

From the Renaissance to the close of the nineteenth century it was customary to accept one of these styles—naturalism—as an absolute standard. All other styles were regarded as barbarous aberrations, whose cause could only be ignorance and lack of skill; it was inconceivable that artists should have violated the canons of naturalism except as the result of a low level of cultural development. Franz Wickhoff, a well-known Austrian art historian of the old school, called nonnaturalistic art the "charming, childlike stammering of stylization." [15] This was the dominant opinion at the time Worringer's book was written, although the hegemony of naturalism had already begun to lose its power over the artists themselves; and Worringer applies himself to the task of dethroning naturalism as an absolute and eternal aesthetic standard.

To do so, Worringer employs the concept of *Kunstwollen*, or will-to-art, which had been developed in the extremely influential writings of another Austrian scholar, Alois Riegl. Riegl had argued that the impulse to creation in the plastic arts was not primarily an urge toward the imitation of the organic world. Instead, he postulated what he called an absolute will-to-art, or better still, will-to-form. This absolute will-to-form is the element common to all activity in the plastic arts, but it cannot be identified with any particular style. All styles, as a matter of fact, express this will-to-form in diverse fashions throughout the course of history. The importance of this idea is that it shifts the center of gravity in the study of style away from mechanical causation (the state of technical artistic knowledge at the time the style flourished) to a causality based on human will, feeling, and response. "The stylistic peculiarities of past epochs," Worringer writes, "are, therefore, not to be explained by lack of ability, but by a differently directed volition."[16] Nonnaturalism cannot be explained as a grotesquely unsuccessful attempt to reproduce natural appearances; nor should it be judged as if it were attempting to compete with naturalism on the latter's own terms. Both types of art were created to satisfy differing spiritual needs and can only be understood if we examine the climates of feeling responsible for the predominance of one or the other at different times.

The heart of Worringer's book consists in his discussion of the spiritual conditions which impel the will-to-art to move in the direction of either naturalism or its opposite. Naturalism, Worringer points out, always has been created by cultures that have achieved an equilibrium between man and the cosmos. Like the Greeks of the classical period, man feels himself at one with organic nature; or, like modern man from the Renaissance to the close of the nineteenth century, he is convinced of his ability to dominate and control natural forces. In both these periods man has a relationship of confidence and intimacy with a world in which he feels at home; and he creates a naturalistic art that delights in reproducing the forms and appearances of the organic world. Worringer warns us, however, not to confuse this delight in the organic with a mere impulse toward imitation. Such imitation is a by-product of naturalism, not its cause. What we enjoy is not the imitation per se but our heightened sense of active harmony with the organic crystallized in the creation or apprehension of a naturalistic work of art.

On the other hand, when the relationship between man and the cosmos is one of disharmony and disequilibrium, we find that nonorganic, linear-geometric styles are always produced. To primitive peoples, for example, the external world is an incomprehensible chaos, a meaningless or terrifying confusion of occurrences and sensations; hence they would hardly take pleasure in depicting this world in their art. Living as they do in a universe of fear, the representation of its features would merely intensify their sense of anguish. Accordingly, their will-to-art goes in the opposite direction: it reduces the appearances of the natural world to linear-geometric forms. Such forms have the stability, the harmony, and the sense of order that primitive man cannot find in the flux of phenomena as—to use a phrase of Hart Crane's—they "plunge in silence by."

At a higher level of cultural development, nonnaturalistic styles like Byzantine and Romanesque are produced during periods dominated by a religion that rejects the natural world as a realm of evil and imperfection.

Instead of depicting the profuse vitality of nature with all its temptations, the will-to-art turns toward spiritualization; it eliminates mass and corporeality and tries to approximate the eternal, ethereal tranquillity of otherworldly existence. In both instances—the primitive and the transcendental—the will-to-art, in response to the prevalent climate of feeling, diverges from naturalism to create aesthetic forms that will satisfy the spiritual needs of their creators. Such forms are always characterized by an emphasis on linear-geometric patterns, on the disappearance of modeling and the attempt to capture the illusion of space, on the dominance of the plane in all types of plastic art.

VII. The Meaning of Spatial Form

The relevance of Worringer's views to modern developments in the plastic arts hardly requires any elaborate commentary. If there is one theme that dominates the history of modern culture since the last quarter of the nineteenth century, it is precisely that of insecurity, instability, the feeling of loss of control over the meaning and purpose of life amidst the continuing triumphs of science and technics. Artists are always the most sensitive barometers of cultural change; and it is hardly surprising that the stylistic evolution of modern art, when viewed as a whole, should reveal the effects of this spiritual crisis. But, as T. E. Hulme was one of the first to realize, aesthetic form in modern literature could be expected to undergo a similar change in response to the same climate of feeling; and Hulme's most interesting essay, *Romanticism and Classicism*, is an attempt to define this change as it affects literary form.

Regrettably, Hulme's notion of aesthetic form in literature was not very clearly worked out, and he mistakenly identified his own problem with the attack on Romanticism made by French neoclassic critics like Charles Maurras and Pierre Lasserre. These writers, who also exercised a strong influence on Irving Babbitt, had bitterly criticized the French Romantics on every conceivable ground; but what most impressed Hulme was their violent denunciation of Romantic subjectivity, their rejection of the unrestrained emotionalism that the Romantics sometimes fobbed off as literature. In reading Worringer, Hulme had remarked that nonnaturalistic styles suppressed the organic, which could also mean the personal and the subjective; and this, he thought, gave him the clue to the new and corresponding style in modern literature.

Accordingly, he announced that the new style in literature would also be impersonal and objective, or at least would not be "like pouring a pot of treacle over the dinner table." It would have a "dry hardness," the hardness of Pope and Horace, as against "the sloppiness which doesn't consider that a poem is a poem unless it is moaning or whining about something or other." "I prophesy," Hulme concludes, "that a period of dry, hard, classical verse is coming."[17]

From Hulme's own poetry we know that he was thinking of something resembling Imagism rather than the later influence of Donne and the Metaphysicals. Moreover, while his prophecy may seem to have struck remarkably close to home, his adoption of the time-honored classic-romantic antithesis could only confuse the issue. Hulme's great merit lies in having been among the first to realize that literary form would undergo a change similar to changes in the plastic arts; but he failed to define this literary form with any exactitude.

Let us go back to Worringer, and, by combining his ideas with those of Lessing, see if we can take up where Hulme's happy but fragmentary intuitions left off.

Since literature is a time-art, we shall take our point of departure from Worringer's discussion of the disappearance of depth (and hence of the world in which time occurs) in nonnaturalistic styles. "It is precisely space," writes Worringer, "which, filled with atmospheric air, linking things together and destroying their individual closedness, gives things their temporal value and draws them into the cosmic interplay of phenomena." [18] Depth, the projection of three-dimensional space, gives objects a time-value because it places them in the real world in which events occur. Now time is the very condition of that flux and change from which, as we have seen, man wishes to escape when he is in a relation of disequilibrium with the cosmos; hence nonnaturalistic styles shun the dimension of depth and prefer the plane. If we look only at the medium of the plastic arts, it is, then, absolutely spatial when compared with literature. But if we look at the relation of form and content, it is thus possible to speak of the plastic arts as being more or less spatial in the course of their history. Paradoxically, this means that the plastic arts have been most spatial when they did not represent the space dimension and least spatial when they did.

In a nonnaturalistic style, then, the inherent spatiality of the plastic arts is accentuated by the effort to remove all traces of time-value. And since modern art is nonnaturalistic, we can say that it is moving in the direction of increased spatiality. The significance of spatial form in modern literature now becomes clear; it is the exact complement in literature, on the level of aesthetic form, to the developments that have taken place in the plastic arts. Spatial form is the development that Hulme was looking for but did not know how to find. In both artistic mediums, one naturally spatial and the other naturally temporal, the evolution of aesthetic form in the twentieth century has been absolutely identical. For if the plastic arts from the Renaissance onward attempted to compete with literature by perfecting the means of narrative representation, then contemporary literature is now striving to rival the spatial apprehension of the plastic arts in a moment of time. Both contemporary art and literature have, each in its own way, attempted to overcome the time elements involved in their structures.

In a purely formal sense, therefore, we have demonstrated the complete congruity of aesthetic form in modern art with the form of modern literature. Thus we have laid bare what Worringer would call the "psychological" roots of spatial form in modern literature. But for a true psychology of style, as Worringer remarks in his *Form in Gothic*, the "formal value" must be shown "to be an accurate expression of the inner value, in such a way that duality of form and content ceases to exist."[19] Hence we must still discuss the relation between spatial form and the content of modern literature, and make some effort to resolve the duality to which Worringer refers.

In the case of Proust, we have already shown that his use of spatial form arose from an attempt to communicate the extratemporal quality of his revelatory moments. Ernst Robert Curtius, at the conclusion of one of the best studies of Proust, has rightly called him a Platonist; for his ultimate value, like that of Plato, was an existence wrenched free from all submission to the flux of the temporal.[20] Proust, as we have seen, was fully alive to the philosophic implications of his own work;

and by explaining these implications for us in his analysis of the revelatory moment, Proust himself indicated the relationship between form and content in his great novel.

With the other writers, however, the problem is more complex. Proust had been primarily concerned with a private and personal experience whose extension to other lives was only implicit; but Pound, Eliot, and Joyce all move out beyond the personal into the wider reaches of history—all deal, in one way or another, with the clash of historical perspectives induced by the identification of modern figures and events with various historical or mythological prototypes. This is quite clear in the *Cantos, The Waste Land,* and in *Ulysses,* where the chief source of meaning is the sense of ironic dissimilarity and yet of profound human continuity between the modern protagonists and their long-dead (or only imaginary) exemplars. A similar palimpsest effect is found in *Nightwood,* where Dr. O'Connor is continually drawing on his "prehistoric memory" for images and metaphors, weaving in the past with the present and identifying the two; and where, even apart from his monologues, the characters are seen in terms of images that depict them as historical embodiments of certain permanent and ahistorical human attitudes.

Allen Tate, in his penetrating essay on the *Cantos,* writes that Ezra Pound's "powerful juxtapositions of the ancient, the Renaissance, and the modern worlds reduce all three elements to an unhistorical miscellany, timeless and without origin."[21] This is called "the peculiarly modern quality of Mr. Pound"; but it is also the "peculiarly modern quality" of all the works we have been considering. They all maintain a continual juxtaposition between aspects of the past and the present so that both are fused in one comprehensive view. Both Tiresias and Dr. O'Connor are focuses of consciousness precisely because they transcend historical limits and encompass all times; the same is true of the unspecified voice intoning the *Cantos*. Leopold Bloom and the other major characters in *Ulysses* are projected in the same fashion; but Joyce, true to the traditions of literary naturalism, refuses to make even the central figure of Bloom more than the *unconscious* bearer of his own immortality.

By this juxtaposition of past and present, as Allen Tate realized, history becomes ahistorical. Time is no longer felt as an objective, causal progression with clearly marked-out differences between periods; now it has become a continuum in which distinctions between past and present are wiped out. And here we have a striking parallel with the plastic arts. Just as the dimension of depth has vanished from the sphere of visual creation, so the dimension of historical depth has vanished from the content of the major works of modern literature. Past and present are apprehended spatially, locked in a timeless unity that, while it may accentuate surface differences, eliminates any feeling of sequence by the very act of juxtaposition. Ever since the Renaissance, modern man has cultivated both the objective visual imagination (the ability to portray space) and the objective historical imagination (the ability to locate events in chronological time); both have now been abandoned.

What has occurred, at least so far as literature is concerned, may be described as the transformation of the historical imagination into myth—an imagination for which historical time does not exist and which sees the actions and event of a particular time only as the bodying forth of eternal prototypes. The historian of religion, Mircea Eliade, has recently noted in modern thought "a resistance to history, a revolt against historical *time,* an attempt to restore this historical time, freighted as it is with human experience, to a place in the time that is cosmic, cyclical, and infinite. In any case," he adds, "it is worth noting that the work of two of the most significant writers of our day—T. S. Eliot and James Joyce—is saturated with nostalgia for the myth of eternal repetition and, in the last analysis, for the abolition of time."[22] These observations from another discipline confirm the view that modern literature has been engaged in transmuting the time world of history into the timeless world of myth. And it is this timeless world of myth, forming the content of so much of modern literature, that finds its appropriate aesthetic expression in spatial form.[23]

Notes

1. André Gide, *Prétextes* (Paris, 1913), 42.
2. This statement is much less true now than it was forty-five years ago when first written. The past half-century has seen a notable increase in studies concerned with the space- and time-aspects of literature and art. As Wellek and Warren have remarked, this was initially attributable to the influence of Existentialist philosophy. For further references, see R. Wellek and A. Warren, *Theory of Literature* (New York, 1956), 264.
3. Ezra Pound, *Make It New* (London, 1934), 336.
4. T. S. Eliot, *Selected Essays* (New York, 1950), 247.
5. R. P. Blackmur, *The Double Agent* (New York, 1935), 49.

6. Maurice Blanchot, "Le Mythe de Mallarmé," *La Part du Feu* (Paris, 1949).

7. Albert Thibaudet, *Gustave Flaubert* (Paris, 1935), 105.

8. Gustave Flaubert, "Correspondence," vol. 3 (1852–1854), 75, *Oeuvres Complètes* (Paris, 1947).

9. Stuart Gilbert, *James Joyce's Ulysses* (New York, 1952); Harry Levin, *James Joyce* (Norfolk, Conn., 1941), 75.

10. Ramon Fernandez, *Messages* (New York, 1927), 210.

11. These remarks were made at least forty-five years ago and very little was then known about the obscure Djuna Barnes. Although my curiosity was piqued, my aim, after all, was not biographical, and I made no serious effort to obtain any further information than I could garner from a quick search of possible sources. It is only recently, on reading the lively book of Andrew Field, *Djuna, The Formidable Miss Barnes* (Austin, Texas, 1985), that I realized what a truly extraordinary person she was and how fascinating her life had been. No one with the slightest interest in Djuna Barnes should neglect to consult Field's book.

12. Fernandez, *Messages*, 158.

13. The best résumé of this movement may be found in Walter Passarge, *Die Philosophie der Kunstgeschichte in der Gegenwart* (Berlin, 1930). A penetrating summary is given by Meyer Schapiro in his article "Style," in *Aesthetics Today*, ed. Morris Philipson (New York, 1961), 81–113.

14. Wilhelm Worringer, *Abstraction and Empathy: A Contribution to the Psychology of Style* (New York, 1953).

15. Ibid., 44.

16. Ibid., 9.

17. T. E. Hulme, *Speculations* (New York, 1924), 113–140.

18. Worringer, *Abstraction and Empathy*, 38.
19. Wilhelm Worringer, *Form in Gothic* (London, 1927), 7.
20. Ernst Robert Curtius, *Französischer Geist im XX. Jahrhundert* (Bern, 1952), 352.
21. Allen Tate, *The Man of Letters in the Modern World* (New York, 1955), 262.
22. Mircea Eliade, *The Myth of the Eternal Return* (New York, 1954), 153.
23. A reader who wishes another perspective on the key issues raised in this essay can find a fair and cogent refutation of my position in Walter Sutton's article, "The Literary Image and the Reader," *Journal of Aesthetics and Art Criticism*, 16, 1 (1957–1958), 112–123.

   Mr. Sutton's objections, however, seem to me to be based on a misunderstanding. His major argument is that, since reading is a time-act, the achievement of spatial form is really a physical impossibility. I could not agree more. But this has not stopped modern writers from working out techniques to achieve the impossible—as much as possible.

2

*S*patial Form:
An Answer to Critics

E v e r since 1945, when my article "Spatial Form in Modern Literature" first appeared, the concept of *spatial form* itself and the analysis of works on which it was based have received wide acceptance in Anglo-American criticism; but they have also elicited a steady drumfire of objections and opposition. When I revised my magazine text for publication in *The Widening Gyre* (1963),[1] I included a brief footnote replying to one critic. Several other essays in that volume also contained reflections provoked by such criticism, though I did not make this relation clear at the time; and I have since regretted not having done so. In any case, I have never otherwise replied to the critics of my argument and point of view.

In recent years, though, there has been a renewed discussion of spatial form and a reconsideration of the merits and deficiencies of the theory as a whole. A new generation, I have become aware, still finds it stimulating and controversial; and I have also become aware that my long silence in the face of criticism has left a number of unanswered questions in the minds of many readers. Hence the time seems opportune to undertake a defense and an explanation that may help to clarify some of the issues at stake. In so doing, I shall retain my original perspective (which essentially saw spatial form as a particular phenomenon of modern avant-garde writing), even though my ideas have since been used by others to apply to a whole range of earlier literature. Such extension, as I now realize, is perfectly legitimate and a welcome widening of my own viewpoint; but I plan to stay within my initial limits for the purpose of this article. I shall defend myself in the context of the avant-garde literature that I initially set out to interpret because, in the first place, this is the context most relevant to the criticisms that have been made; and, in the second, because a more general theory of spatial form involves other problems that overflow the boundaries I have set myself here. I shall discuss them in the next chapter.

Before going on to answer critics of spatial form in detail, it seems to me essential to establish a point that has generally been misunderstood. Far too many readers have assumed that I was a fanatical partisan of experimentalism in all its varieties simply because my attitude towards it was analytical rather than condemnatory and because I tried to understand the moderns in their own terms. Certainly I admired the work of all the writers that I discussed; but, without feeling it necessary to be too self-assertive, I thought that I had made clear that my own attitude was not that of a committed advocate or defender. At the very beginning of my essay, in talking about Lessing, I remarked that I wished to use his ideas solely as descriptive, not at all as normative, categories. "Lessing's insights may be used solely as instruments of analysis, *without proceeding to judge the value of individual works by how closely they adhere to the norms he laid down.* . . . For what Lessing offered was not a new set of opinions but a new conception of aesthetic form" (italics added). These sentences were perhaps not as clear as they might have been, and may have been read to apply only to Lessing's own evaluations; but they were meant to indicate my own position as well and were emphatically *not* intended to imply a positive valuation of modernist works simply because they *violate* Lessing's norms. My aim, like that of Ortega y Gasset in his *Dehumanization of*

Art, was to work out descriptive categories for a new literary phenomenon, not to establish the rules of a modernist critical canon.

All through the essay, as a matter of fact, I kept indicating that I was setting up what Max Weber called an "ideal type"—now called a "model"—rather than describing what was empirically and literally true in any particular case. In speaking, for example, of the "space-logic" of reflexive reference that governed modern poetry, and of the necessity "to suspend the process of individual reference temporarily until the entire pattern of internal references can be apprehended as a unity," I specifically labeled this as the definition of a model. "This explanation, of course," I added in the next sentence, "is the extreme statement of an ideal condition rather than of an actually existing state of affairs." Years later, when I revised the essay for inclusion in *The Widening Gyre*, I unwisely omitted this sentence and replaced it by what I thought would be an unmistakable indication of my continuing skepticism about spatial form *à outrance*. Noting the formal resemblance between Stéphane Mallarmé's *Un Coup de dés, The Waste Land*, and the *Cantos*, I remarked that the ambition of modern poetry to dislocate "the temporality of language . . . has a necessary limit. If pursued with Mallarmé's relentlessness, it culminates in the self-negation of language and the creation of a hybrid pictographic 'poem' that can only be considered a fascinating historical curiosity." Concrete poetry has never seemed to me to have much interest or much future—though I have a sneaking sympathy for its practitioners because I have spent so much time thinking about what they are trying to do.

Similarly, my remarks about various novels (with the exception of *Nightwood*) were by no means intended as readings of these works in any definitive sense, and I assumed my reader would understand that I was focusing only on those formal elements of the work necessary to make clear the "spatiality" of their structure. This did not mean that I thought other aspects of these books inferior, insignificant, or unworthy of notice. Roger Shattuck, whose own writings I greatly admire, has carried on an amicable polemic with me over the years concerning my comments about *A la recherche du temps perdu*. He believes that my exclusive focus on the final "stereoscopic vision" of Proust, the attainment of an extratemporal "spatial" perspective in which the narrator can view his life as a whole, somehow is intended to downgrade all the other multifarious experiences of that life. "But we are dealing with a linear story which Proust carefully and properly called *a search*," Shattuck reminds me. "Far more aptly it could be represented as a climb to the top of the mountain . . . that allows one's gaze to move at will from feature to feature and to take it in all at once. That view is essentially *spatial* (italics added). But it does not and cannot abolish the climb that took one to the summit, and the temporal order of events in that climb."[2]

There is really no quarrel here between Shattuck and myself; we have merely undertaken to do different things, and my narrower point of view was necessitated by my purpose. I can only add that, at the time I wrote, the linear aspects of Proust's search—the social and psychological dimension of his work—had already been amply discussed in the critical literature (after all, I had cut my teeth on *Axel's Castle*); but nobody had quite seen, with as much clarity as I thought necessary, the point I was trying to make. Indeed, almost twenty years later, it was still being hailed as a valuable new insight in France when Georges Poulet published his book on *L'Espace proustien* (which refers to my text). A penetrating discussion by Gérard Genette of "Proust Palimpseste," several years later, informs the reader that "lost time is not, for Proust, as a widely spread misunderstanding would have it, the 'past,' but *time in a pure state*, that is, in fact, by the fusion of an instant of the present with an instant of the past, the contrary of time that flows: *the extra-temporal, eternity*."[3] My limited focus in giving Proust's novel what Genette calls "une lecture structurante" would thus still seem to be an emphasis that has not lost its usefulness.

. . .

What has struck me in general, while reading through the reactions to my article that have accumulated over the years, is how little *specific* objection has been taken to my actual arguments or analyses. Most of the discussion has turned on the larger cultural implications of the artistic tendency represented by my examples, not with what I had to say about them. Only two of my critics, so far as I am aware, dealt with my ideas as such and tried to refute them within the terms I had established.

One of the earliest is G. Giovannini, who is interested in the methodological problem of a comparative study of differing art forms, and who approaches the issue of spatial form from this point of view.[4] Unfortunately, it is a point of view which leads to a total misunderstanding of what I was talking about. Giovannini assumes, for example, that I was influenced by John Peale Bishop, who claimed "that since space (as well as time) is a deeply rooted concept of the mind, it inevitably informs poetic structure." Bishop's article, in the first place, came out simultaneously with my own and could thus hardly have influenced it; in the second, I was not interested in arguing any such general thesis or applying "a method based on the notion of time and space as comparable or quasi-identical" as Giovannini claims. Following Lessing, I very carefully distinguished between the two as *not* comparable but showed that *within* literature, the structure of modern works took on aspects that required them to be apprehended spatially instead of according to the natural temporal order of language.

Giovannini's fundamental error is to take for granted, simply because I began with Lessing, that I was interested in the old *ut pictura poesis* problem and was maintaining that literature could attain the spatial effects of painting. Thus he remonstrates that the "instantaneous fusion of fragments in *The Waste Land*" is not "an imitation of spatial art" (I had never claimed that it was) but rather "a technique of concentration and rapid shift without transitions, a technique which is probably a development of elements within a literary tradition." These words are meant as a criticism because I am supposed to be arguing that Eliot's effects were those of painting; but I was doing no such thing. Giovannini pays no attention whatever to my specific disclaimer on this point, contained in the remark that Pound defines the image "*not as a pictorial reproduction* but as a unification of disparate ideas and emotions into a complex presented spatially in a moment of time" (italics added). As should be clear by now, Giovannini's failure to grasp my ideas is so complete, and his criticisms accordingly so wide of the mark, that there is little point in continuing to discuss them any further.

A much more perceptive critic is Walter Sutton, whose article, "The Literary Image and the Reader," stresses that, since reading is a time-act, the spatialization of literature can never be entirely achieved.[5] Sutton evidently overlooked the qualifications I had made on this point myself; but in any case, as I responded briefly to him in *The Widening Gyre*, "this has not stopped modern writers from working out techniques to achieve the impossible—as much as possible." I think it will be instructive, though, to consider his arguments a little more at length on this occasion.

One of his major criticisms is directed against my remarks on the "space-logic" of modern poetry, and my contention that readers are required to suspend the process of denotational reference temporarily until the entire pattern of *internal* references can be apprehended as a unity. But what, he asks, "is going on in the mind of the reader during the process of reading? . . . Presumably nothing, since consciousness in time has somehow been suspended." On the basis of this last (but totally unwarranted) inference from my text, Sutton triumphantly concludes that such a "*nothing* is inconceivable. We are in a realm beyond criticism, beyond theory." Certainly we should be if I had really implied that *nothing* was going on in the mind of the reader of modern poetry; but I had made no such nonsensical assumption. I stated what has become a platitude—and what I can now put in more precise linguistic terminology—that the synchronic relations *within* the text take precedence over diachronic referentiality, and that it is only after the pattern of synchronic relations has been grasped as a unity that the "meaning" of the poem can be understood. Naturally, to work out such synchronic relations involves the time-act of reading; but the temporality of this act is no longer coordinated with the dominant structural elements of the text. Temporality becomes, as it were, a purely physical limit of apprehension, which conditions but does not determine the work and whose expectations are thwarted and superseded by the space-logic of synchronicity.

Another of Sutton's objections is leveled against my assertion that, in the poetry of Eliot and Pound, "syntactical sequence is given up for a structure depending upon the perception of relationships between disconnected word-groups" (i.e., a structure of juxtaposition rather than of sequence). "In all cases," he retorts, "one could hardly say that there is no relationship in time of the *apparently* dissociated images of these poems. Their relationship in time is in fact the concern of the poet"; and Sutton points to the ironic contrast between Prufrock and Hamlet, as well as the "contrast between the classic past and the vulgarized present in Pound's 'Mauberley,'" to prove his point. It is clear here that Sutton and I are simply talking about different things: he is referring to the *thematic* meaning conveyed by the time-contrasts in the poetry, while I am speaking of the temporality of *language*. The time-contrasts he mentions emerge, all the same, from the juxtaposition of word-groups syntactically unrelated to each other, which means that significance is no longer determined by linguistic sequence.

Such thematic use of time-contrasts returns at the end of Sutton's article, in a more relevant context, when he takes issue with my contention that spatial form can be correlated with the substitution of the mythical for the historical imagination. "I must particularly disagree with Mr. Frank's statement," he says, "because works like *The Waste Land* and the *Cantos* and *Nightwood* are so obviously works of the historical imagination—of a skeptical, self-conscious awareness of the predicament of modern man as a victim of cultural decay." Sutton here neglects to inform the reader that I made this very point myself, and spoke of the source of meaning in the *Cantos, The Waste Land,* and *Ulysses* as being "*the sense of ironic dissimilarity* and yet of profound human continuity between the modern protagonists and their long-dead (or only imaginary) exemplars" (italics added). But I argued that, by yoking past and present together in this way, these contrasts were felt as "locked in a timeless unity (that), *while it may accentuate surface differences,* eliminates any feeling of sequence by the very act of juxtaposition" (italics added).

There is thus no argument here about the immediate impact of these works in creating an ironic sense of contrast between past and present; but Sutton denies the deeper meaning that seemed to me implicit in their formal novelty—the "profound human continuity" that they took for granted. To buttress my position I can cite some words of Eliot himself, who, in the same year he wrote *The Waste Land* (1921), saw a performance of *Le Sacre du printemps* given by the Ballets Russes. This work, he observed, "brought home . . . *the continuity of the human predicament:* primitive man on the dolorous steppes, modern man in the city with its despairing noises, *the essential problem unchanging.*" [6] Such is the feeling underlying the shock effects of the contrast in all the texts I spoke about; and I was concerned to disengage this latent ahistoricity contained in what seemed a skeptical and self-conscious historical imagination. Certainly the latter was there; but it was striving to transform itself into myth.

The great works of modernism are thus analogous, it seems to me, to those examples of medieval sculpture or book illustrations, in which figures from the Old and New Testaments, classical antiquity, and sometimes local history are all grouped together as part of one timeless complex of significance. Erich Auerbach has explained the assumptions underlying such significance in his famous article, "Figura";[7] but while no such unified system of meanings and values exists for the moderns, they strive to attain a similar effect in purely formal terms.

As Sergei Eisenstein has pointed out, the juxtaposition of disparate images in a cinematic montage automatically creates a synthesis of meaning between them; and this supersedes any sense of temporal discontinuity.[8] More recently, Alain Robbe-Grillet made the same point in speaking of the lack of time-depth in his novels: "The cinema knows only a single grammatical modality: the present of the indicative."[9] The juxtaposition of disparate historical images in Joyce, Pound, and Eliot also transforms the past into the present of the indicative; and in doing so they turn history into myth (Ernst Cassirer defines the mythical imagination precisely in terms of the lack of a "dimension of depth," a lack of differentiation between foreground and background in its pictures of reality).[10] One has only to compare this with, for example, the classical historical novel, to feel the difference immediately. For this characteristic nineteenth-century genre stressed the *pastness* of the past, the gulf created by historical time that separates the world of the novel irrevocably from the present of the reader, or which clarifies the process of transition from one to the other. It is amusing to see Sutton illustrating my point, while thinking to refute it, by his remark that Eliot's image of Mr. Eugenides, the commercial traveler from Smyrna, is "the debased modern counterpart of the ancient trader who brought the mysteries of the fertility cults to the

West." Exactly: he is part of the same timeless pattern in a different guise.

• • •

For the most part, as I have said, the criticisms directed against spatial form have been aimed not so much at the concept itself and my discussion of it as at the kind of literature that it helps to explain and, presumably, to justify. This is certainly the case with Philip Rahv's influential essay, "The Myth and the Powerhouse," which is invariably cited among the most powerful criticisms of spatial form.[11] Rahv was greatly incensed by the rise in prestige of myth as a focus of cultural attention, and he set out to deflate it as a valid response to the acute sense of cultural crisis that he freely acknowledged to exist. He cites the evidence given in my essay as proof of "the turn from history toward myth" that he deplores; he remarks that *Finnegans Wake*, which I had not mentioned at all, "is the most complete example of 'spatial form' in modern literature"; and he concedes that "Joseph Frank's definition of the form is extremely plausible." No argument is made that my analysis does not accurately grasp the modern situation; but Rahv nonetheless opposes it on other grounds.

One is that "he [Frank] too readily assumes that the mythic imagination is actually operative in the writers he examines. But the supplanting of the sense of history by the sense of mythic time is scarcely accomplished with so much ease; the mere absence of the one does not necessarily confirm the presence of the other. For my part, what I perceive in Pound and Eliot are not the workings of the mythic imagination but an aesthetic simulacrum of it, a learned illusion of timelessness."

These sentences baffled me for some time because I could not quite grasp of what I was being accused. But they seem to mean that I believed Pound and Eliot to have *literally* reverted to the condition of primitives, to have forgotten all about time and history, and to be truly living in—and writing out of—a mythical imagination untouched by their situation as moderns. In fact, however, this notion is purely a product of Rahv's polemical talent, not of anything I had said. What was I talking about if not precisely "the aesthetic simulacrum" I was supposed to have overlooked? There is no difference between my position and Rahv's own presumably opposing assertion that "they [Pound and Eliot] are as involved in historicism as most contemporary writers sensitive to 'the modern situation,' but in their case the form it takes is negative."

In the remainder of his essay, Rahv does not so much attack spatial form as articulate his dislike of the negative response to history that it expresses. "The fear of history is at bottom the fear of the hazards of freedom. In so far as man can be said to be capable of self-determination, history is the sole sphere in which he can conceivably attain it." What these words really mean, on close scrutiny, is very difficult to decide; if they simply assert that man as a species lives in an empirical world and can act only within its limits, then one can hardly object to such a resounding platitude. Otherwise, they may be taken as the expression of a personal position about which there is very little to say—except that the greatest modern writers have felt quite the opposite and that Rahv's animadversions hardly help us to understand why. One would have to be either a fool (which Rahv most emphatically was not) or a fanatic to claim that, after the experiences of the first three-quarters of the

twentieth century, there are no good grounds for refusing to worship before the Moloch of "history" in the old
starry-eyed nineteenth-century fashion, with its built-in
theological postulates. Claude Lévi-Strauss has neatly
exposed the intellectual naiveté of such a blind faith in
history in his polemic with Sartre (*La Pensée sauvage*);
and we now see such faith as part of the same Western
ethnocentrism that Worringer discarded long ago as a
criterion for the plastic arts. It is time to stop allowing
the same position to influence our discussion of literature as well.

To return to literature, however, the implication of
Rahv's words, very simply, is that modern writers should
not employ forms that negate history and time. But he
was too sophisticated a critic and polemicist, and perhaps too much a genuine admirer of modern literature,
to express such a position overtly. Instead, he skir-
mished with spatial form so as to avoid the considerable
embarrassment of having to attack Pound, Joyce, Eliot,
et al., and thus end up sounding like the veriest Philis-
tine (or, perish the thought, Irving Babbitt or Paul Elmer
More). Rahv's problem was that he was unable to reconcile his literary taste with his ideological convictions;
and while this inconsistency does him honor (it was the
source of his great services to Anglo-American literature
as editor of *Partisan Review*), its result is to make his polemic with spatial form inconsequent and unconvincing. What it expresses is really a visceral opposition to
modernism as a whole that his own critical judgment refused to allow to gain the upper hand; and in attacking
critics rather than writers he found some relief from the
pressure of his internal contradiction.

Rahv's commitment to "history" clearly derived from
his residual Marxism; and a much more detailed attack

on spatial form, using almost the same terms, can accordingly be found in a book that seems to have escaped general notice. It is, as a matter of fact, a quite valuable book, written by the East German Anglicist Robert Weimann and called "*New Criticism*" *und die Entwicklung Bürgerlicher Literaturwissenschaft* (1962). Weimann's work is very well informed and contains one of the best historical accounts I am familiar with of the background, origins, and theories of the Anglo-American New Criticism; but since he writes as an orthodox Marxist, his attitude is inevitably hostile. Nonetheless, the tradition of German *Gründlichkeit* rescues the book from being simply a partisan polemic and gives it independent value. A special section is devoted to the analysis of the New Critical theory of the novel, and, in a separate chapter, spatial form is discussed under the title: "The Negation of the Art of Narrative."

Weimann expounds the main lines of the essay quite faithfully and even, at times, with accents of appreciation. After quoting my description of spatial form in *Ulysses*, for example, he says: "As a contribution to the interpretation of the so-called *avant-garde* novel, this may not be without justification. Frank, who relies primarily on examples of this kind, is able in this way to analyze Joyce's work and his 'unbelievably laborious fragmentation of narrative structure.'" What Weimann objects to is not the insight offered by such analysis, but rather what he calls "the apologetic tendency" that he detects in the essay. "Like other interpreters of modern bourgeois prose," he writes, "Frank also sees 'not only a history of dissolution and destruction, but one of creative discovery and achievement'" (the phrase in single quotes is from the German critic Fritz Martini). So far as I do not regard modern experiments in the novel as *ipso facto* a sign of creative decadence, this is unquestionably true; though I should wish to add that there are as many mediocre experimentalists as banal naturalists and that I do not think literary quality simply a matter of adopting this or that technique. Weimann wishes to prove, however, that I set up fragmentization of narrative and temporality as positive aesthetic qualities that become a critical norm; and this gives him a bit of trouble.

He manages, though, by taking a passage completely out of context and interpreting it in a way that is quite misleading. Early in the essay, expounding the implicit assumptions of the poetics of the image, I remarked that "if the chief value of an image was its capacity to present an intellectual and emotional complex simultaneously, linking up images would clearly destroy most of their efficacy." To an impartial reader, it should be perfectly clear that I was simply developing the immanent logic of the aesthetics of the image; but Weimann finds it polemically useful to turn my remark into a value judgment. "Because the New Critic affirms *only* the atemporal and fragmentized, that is, autonomous *image*, temporality and sequence in the novel are labelled as a lack of 'efficacy.'" From here it is quite easy for Weimann to accuse the New Critics—impersonated by myself—of having constructed an aesthetics of the novel "conceived as an apologetic for imperialistic artistic decadence."

Weimann, all the same, has a clear and honest position, which allows him to state the issues without equivocation and, unlike Rahv, to take a consistent stand. Despite his obvious moral distaste for *Nightwood* ("homosexuality and sodomy are merely two links in a long chain of human aberrations"), he is quite capable of agreeing that my "spatial" conception "finds in Djuna Barnes's experimental novel . . . a not uninteresting self-confirmation." But of course Weimann staunchly refused to acknowledge the *legitimacy* of any such experimentation and objects to the modernist *mélange des genres*, which, as he rightly sees, has substituted lyric for narrative principles of organization in the novel. Like so many other partisans of "history," who believe that their devotion to time and change entitles them to strike poses of moral superiority, Weimann also paradoxically hangs on for dear life to the immutability and virginal inviolability of the literary genres. Everything else in human life is supposed to be transformed from top to bottom in the name of "progress," and humankind is invited (ordered?) to participate in the mutation with whoops of joy, but hands off the sacrosanct rules of narrative art! "The loss of the temporal dimension," he writes warningly, "means the destruction of the specific narrative effect, namely, the representation of temporal processes, development, mutations, changes, etc." And this is reprehensible because, "in back of the aesthetic negation of narrative stands the ideological negation of *self-transforming reality*, the negation of the historicity of our world." Like Rahv, Weimann also thinks it is morally inadmissible for mankind, even if it prefers to do so, to take refuge in art from "historicity"; and the Russians, who at least have the courage of their convictions, brought out bulldozers (in the pre-Gorbachovian years) to break up outdoor exhibitions of abstract art by their younger painters, who were curiously indifferent to the glories and achievements of the historical process.[12]

. . .

Of all the attacks on spatial form over the years, by far the most interesting, subtle, and critically productive has been that by Frank Kermode. Kermode is unquestionably one of the best critics now writing in English; his works exhibit a responsiveness and sensitivity to the passing scene, a wide-ranging intellectual curiosity, and an unerring instinct for the major problems that few contemporaries can match. From the very first moment that he embarked on his career as a critic—from the moment that he left Renaissance scholarship to emerge as the most interesting and provocative analyst of modernism in English—he has been concerned with issues that culminate in his rejection of spatial form. Indeed, after reading most of his relevant work, it seems to me that, even if the theory itself were proven worthless, it would still have been of value in providing some of the stimulus for Frank Kermode to have written *The Sense of an Ending*. But of course I do not think the theory worthless; I think, rather, that Kermode, in opposing it as strenuously as he does, is operating under something of a delusion; in reality, by the time he had finished his book, he had accepted everything about spatial form except the terminology. Let me see if I can justify this conviction and also offer some reason for the puzzling *space-shyness* (to adapt a term of Worringer's) that he continues to exhibit.

Frank Kermode's first important work, *The Romantic Image* (1957), is a delightful and original exploration, full of piquant detail about French music-hall dancers, devoted to the historical background of what he calls the Romantic-Symbolist tradition in English literature, that is, the tradition of modernism, whose roots go back to Blake and Coleridge, and whose career he traces up through Pater, Yeats (the key figure), and the twentieth-century modernists Eliot and Pound. This tradition, as Kermode ably defines it, turned the artist into the purveyor of some sort of irrational wisdom supposedly

superior to commonsense knowledge and reason; it isolated him from the world and the ordinary concerns of
men; and its ideal was to overcome the dissociation of
thought and feeling which, in modern culture, had resulted from the rise of science and rationalism and the
triumph of the latter over religion and tradition. The
Dancer became so important a symbol in this aesthetic
because, in the expressive human body, this dissociation is healed; some sort of revelation, some sort of
gleam of what Mallarmé called "l'incorporation univer-
selle de l'idée," is accomplished through the spectacle of
dance. The same is true of music, whose purity, according to Pater and also earlier to Schopenhauer, all the arts
aspire to emulate and attain. The ideal of this aesthetic is
a nondiscursive art, breaking with ordinary life and its
trivial concerns, aristocratic and elitist in relation to
plebeian mortals, seeking to rise above what Kermode
calls, in a typical phrase, "the ordinary syntax of the
daily life of action." Implicit in modernism, he finds, is
the desire "to recover those images of truth which have
nothing to do with the intellect of scientists, *nothing to
do with time*" (italics added).

Kermode's attitude to this movement, which he de-
picts so well, was fluctuating and ambiguous, composed of that mixture of attachment and withdrawal
that he holds up as one of the chief virtues of Edmund
Wilson, a critic he very much admires. It would have
been impossible for Kermode to have written so well of
Yeats without the attachment; but the withdrawal is
equally evident when he attacks Eliot's theory of a "dissociation of sensibility" as lacking any historical grounding and indicates his distaste for the divorce of art from
life and of poetic meaning from ordinary discourse. He
speaks admiringly of Yvor Winters's assault on the

Romantic-Symbolist tradition and considers one of "the main issues of modern poetic" to be "the unformulated quarrel between the orthodoxy of symbolism and the surviving elements of the empirical-utilitarian tradition which, we are assured, is characteristically English." It is a pity, he says, that "the movement of the thirties away from aesthetic monism, the new insistence on the right to discourse, even to say such things as 'We must love one another or die' (as Auden does in an exquisite poem) has ceased." Well aware that the Romantic-Symbolist tradition was still dominant, he nonetheless looks forward, in conclusion, to the end of its reign and the restoration of Milton and Spenser to the central position from which they had been dethroned. For, once that has been accomplished, "the dissociation of sensibility, the great and in some ways noxious historical myth of symbolism (though the attempt to see history in terms of the Image was noble) will be forgotten."

Kermode's attitude to the Romantic-Symbolist tradition, as we see, is both reverential and dismissive; it performed a noble function in its time, but its time has passed, and it should now be interred with full military honors. The reason is not so much literary—because Kermode prefers long poems to short ones or wishes poetry again to appeal to the common reader—but rather, it seems to me, practical and "empirical-utilitarian." The new poetic that he looks forward to, he explains, "would be remote from the radicalism of Blake, have little to do with the forlorn hopes of Mallarmé, and less with the disastrous *dérèglement* of Rimbaud. *We have perhaps learnt to respect order, and felt on our bodies the effect of irrationalism, at any rate when the sphere of action is invaded by certain elements of the Romantic rêve*" (italics added). It is this translation of the Romantic-Symbolist tradition into the realm of action, the application of its irrationalism to the sphere of life and politics, that finally accounts for Kermode's hostility. The term "spatial" is used once in the book, and then only in a glancing reference to the "holistic" criticism of G. Wilson Knight; but opposition to what the word designates lurks in the background nonetheless. For we should remember that Kermode has identified the Romantic-Symbolist hostility to the intellect of the scientists—that is, the *source* of its irrationalism—with the effort to escape from time.

· · ·

As we come to *The Sense of an Ending* (1966) from this earlier book, we hear, as the French say, an entirely different *son de cloche*. A great change has occurred, and it may confidently be attributed to Kermode's fascination with that quintessential Romantic-Symbolist poet, Wallace Stevens, to whom, in the interim, he had devoted an excellent little book.[13] In any case, there is no longer any talk, in *The Sense of an Ending*, about the ordinary reader, poetry as discourse, or the empirical-utilitarian tradition. Man now lives in a world whose contours are provided not by the intellect of the scientists, but by the myths of Crisis, Apocalypse, Decadence, and the End and by the existential need to give shape and pattern to the unendurable meaninglessness of pure temporal duration. Just as, according to Wallace Stevens, the poetic imagination projects its metaphors on bare materiality to endow nature with metaphysical significance, so the imagination of Western man, living in the rectilinear time of a crumbling Judeo-Christian civilization, projects the myths of his religion onto the course of events and locates within such structures the meaning of his own life.

What is striking about all this, from my point of view, is not so much Kermode's change of intellectual front (probably less radical than I make it out to be) but rather the shift in attitude towards time that it illustrates. Time, for the earlier Kermode, had been something unproblematic and taken for granted; it was part of the world defined by the intellect of the scientists and known to the ordinary man (though the two are scarcely the same). To live uncomplicatedly in time, though, was to escape the temptations of the Romantic *rêve* and also to resist the danger of translating its irrationalism into action. But Kermode has since learnt that man's relation to time is much more complex; experimental psychology has persuaded him that we say *tick-tock* because to repeat *tick-tick* endlessly is a burden that humans cannot bear; where there is a beginning, we want an end, a human pattern, the music of the spheres, not simply the hum and buzz of repetition *ad infinitum*. The intolerable time of sheer chronicity creates a problem that humanity has had to cope with since the beginning of *its* time; and humanity has done so either in the myths of its religions or, when such "supreme fictions" no longer inspire faith, in the secular fictions of art and literature. Myths are thus fictions that one believes to be true, and which inspire actual behavior; fictions are what we know as works of art, whose definition has always been that we are aware of their status as being fictive, a seeming, an illusion, *Schein*—or, if we are positivist, downright lies.

This distinction is a very important one for Kermode because it helps him out of an extremely ticklish dilemma. No longer able to rely on the intellect of the scientists as a criterion of truth and, as he had once done, using it as a weapon to demolish the dangerous fantasies of the Romantic *rêve*, he feels exposed to the charge

of now accepting all the irrationalisms he had once casti-
gated so vehemently and so justifiably. And indeed, if
what gives meaning to human life is simply one or another myth, how is one to choose between those com-
peting for the allegiance of the modern mind? "If *King
Lear* is an image of the promised end," Kermode writes
with commendable candor, "so is Buchenwald"; "both
stand under the accusation of being horrible, rootless
fantasies, the one no more true or more false than the
other." Kermode rather evades this issue of the rela-
tivity of values instead of meeting it head-on, though it
would be unfair to criticize him for having adopted a
flanking strategy—the greatest modern minds all leave
us equally in the lurch at this point. But he copes with it,
in his own way, by the distinction between myth and
fiction. "Fictions can degenerate into myths whenever
they are not consciously held to be fictive. In this sense
anti-Semitism is a degenerate fiction, a myth; and *Lear* is
a fiction." There would seem to be no ambiguity about
these terms and what Kermode means by them; so long
as we remain within the realm of art, so long as fictions
remain *conscious* fictions, we do not have to worry about
myth and its dangers.

I shall return to this important point and examine
how Kermode uses (or abuses) it, in a moment; but first
I should like to focus on what seems to me the most
fruitful insight in his book. This insight is that the plots
of our literature are, to a great extent, dependent on the
pattern of expectations established by the apocalyptic
and eschatological imagination of our culture, and that
they can be seen to have developed out of this pattern.
Using the language of theology, Kermode points out
that plots presuppose "that an end will bestow upon [a]
whole duration and meaning. . . . Within this orga-

nization that which was conceived of as simply successive becomes charged with past and future; what was *chronos* becomes *kairos*" (meaning, by this latter term, the meeting of past and future in a present which Kermode calls "historical moments of intemporal significance"). Elsewhere, he speaks of plots as being the "purging" of "mere successiveness . . . by the establishment of a significant relation between the moment and a remote origin and end, by a concord of past, present, and future." Plots therefore seem to work *against* the flow of time and to keep alive, or to create, an indigenous kind of unity that overarches and reshapes the constraints of pure temporal linearity.

One can imagine an innocent reader, ignorant both of Kermode's intellectual history and of the terminological warfare of contemporary criticism, thinking it perfectly appropriate to conclude that plots thus exhibit a tendency to counteract time by "spatializing" its flow, that is, to create relations of meaning detached from pure succession. To be sure, in most literary works before the mid-twentieth century (the great exception, of course, being *Tristram Shandy*), such plot relationships remain in the background and are firmly subordinate to temporal continuity; but Kermode has performed a very valuable service in pointing out their nature as embryonic nonlinear structures. However, he rejects with great decisiveness any idea of using such a term as "spatial" to characterize these forms. "Such concords," he says, "can easily be called 'time-defeating,' but the objection to that word is that it leads directly to the questionable critical practice of calling literary structures *spatial*. This is a *critical fiction* that has regressed into a *myth* because it was not discarded at the right moment in the argument [italics added in last sentence]. 'Timeredeeming' is a better word, perhaps." Nor is this the only passage in which Kermode breaks a lance against the use of these terms; similar statements can be found all through his book.

Somewhat later, for example, he speaks of St. Augustine reciting his psalm, in which "he found . . . a figure for the integration of past, present, and future which defies successive time. He discovered what is now erroneously referred to as 'spatial form.'" Rather than use this latter term, Kermode prefers to reach back to Thomas Aquinas and resurrect his concept of *aevum*. This is a word for the time of the angels, neither the eternity of God nor the transience of mere mortals; a duration out of time but which, as it were, coexists with it. "It [the *aevum*]," Kermode assures us, "does not abolish time or spatialize it"—as if the latter term meant the abolition of time entirely, although I employed it only to refer to the same sort of "intemporal" *organization* of temporality that Kermode analyzes. Despite his efforts, however, he does not succeed entirely in freeing his own ideas from "spatial" contamination. For he later speaks of Spenser's poetic use of the "time-defeating *aevum*"; and in distinguishing between the older moderns and the newer generation, who revive the lineage of Dada and Surrealism, he remarks: "But they (the men of 1914) were intellectuals and space-men, not time-men with a special interest in the chaotic present." If so, then why protest so strenuously against using "spatial" terms in reference to their work?

Questions of terminology are of course insignificant, and I am much more interested in the obvious analogies between Kermode's ideas and my own than in arguing on behalf of my particular set of labels. But, all the same, Kermode's stubborn opposition to my terms is rather an odd phenomenon. Why such obsessive hostility to a critical vocabulary? And why, in particular, does such hostility cause him to lose control of his own categories and to misuse them so lamentably? For how, it may be asked, is it possible for a "critical fiction" to regress into a myth? Critical fictions, after all, are literary criticism and refer to literature; nothing at all is said by Kermode, or has been said by those who call some literary structures "spatial" (myself among others), which transfers the argument from the realm of fiction to that of myth as Kermode has defined it (Buchenwald, the Gulag Archipelago, the Second Coming, etc.). Clearly, Kermode's animus against the word "spatial" has loaded it with such an affective charge that he is unable to handle it properly even inside his own framework of ideas. Or rather, what he does, in classic psychoanalytic style, is to project his own animosity onto others and to turn them into scapegoats. For it is he himself who makes spatial form into a "myth," not those whom he accuses of failing to drop the term at the right stage of the argument. It is he who refuses to treat it as a neutral critical fiction, perhaps useful or perhaps not; it is he who fills it with a "mythical" content that finally allows him, in a phrase quite unworthy of his usual fairness and good sense, to speak of "the spatial order of the modern critic or the closed authoritarian society" as if the two really had something in common, and as if to refer to the one necessarily meant to approve of the other.[14]

How is one to account for this intense hostility to the "spatial" that Kermode exhibits to such an alarming degree, which he never justifies or explains, and which causes so lucid a mind to land in such confusion? Why should the critical fiction of spatial form invariably be equated in his book with the myth of fascist totalitarianism?

Part of the answer can no doubt be found in the long-established association in his mind between the "abolition of time" and the practical effects of "irrationalism," which, as we have seen, goes back to *The Romantic Image*. Another link becomes clear in the remainder of the passage from which the above quotation was taken. Here Kermode is talking about the reactionary politics of the Anglo-American moderns (Yeats, Eliot, Pound, Wyndham Lewis); and the last, who at one point openly praised Hitler, quite clearly is his *bête noire*, whom he cannot refer to except in accents of loathing. "He [Lewis] painted on a theory that the closed society of 'abstraction'— an anti-kinetic, anti-humanist society, ruled by fear—much like the fiction of Worringer, was the best for art." And, a bit later, he says that Lewis wanted to get rid of "democracy and all the 'Bergsonian' attitudes to time and human psychology, all the mess which makes up a commonplace modern view of human reality." Lewis, it will be recalled, was the most vigorous and loquacious English champion of "space" and "spatiality" against the time-flux of Bergsonism. It is evidently of Lewis that Kermode thinks whenever these words cross his horizon (gratuitously throwing Worringer into the hateful complex for good measure); and the words thus release the deep-rooted antagonism to Lewis that goes back again to those unforgettable years when fascist "irrationalism" was wreaking its havoc on the modern world.

. . .

It is difficult for me to quarrel with someone for whose feelings I have so much sympathy and whose social-political antipathies I fully share. But just as noble sentiments do not necessarily make good poetry, so admirable moral convictions do not always guarantee infallibility of thought. I should, therefore, merely like to say two things about Kermode's reaction. One is that my own use of "spatial" categories was inspired not by Wyndham Lewis (I had not even read *Time and Western Man* when I wrote my article) but by Lessing, a good Enlightenment liberal, the foe of anti-Semitism, the friend of Moses Mendelssohn, the author of *Nathan der Weise*, etc.; in other words, Kermode's associations are not my own, and there is no reason why his should be accepted as obligatory. Less personally, it is time that English critics overcame their provincialism, took a closer look at the literature of some other countries, and realized that the experimental modernism linked in England with right-wing political sympathies had quite other affiliations elsewhere.

A much more balanced view of this matter has been given by the Mexican poet and critic Octavio Paz, whose *Children of the Mire* is, in my opinion, the most profound recent interpretation of the modern literary situation. "Modern literature," he writes,

> is an impassioned rejection of the modern age. This rejection is no less violent among the poets of Anglo-American "modernism" than among the members of the European and Latin-American avant-gardes. Although the former are reactionaries and the latter revolutionaries, both were anti-capitalist. Their different attitudes originated in a common aversion to the world of the bourgeoisie. . . . Like their Romantic and Symbolist predecessors, twentieth-century poets have set against the linear time of progress and history the instantaneous time of eroticism or the cyclical time of

analogy or the hollow time of the ironic consciousness. Image and humor: rejections of the chronological time of critical reason and its deification of the future.[15]

It is no longer permissible, it seems to me, for English critics never to take account of other "modernisms" in elaborating their views. It is really no longer permissible to identify the revolt against linear time in modern literature as a whole—a revolt which has led to the experimental techniques analyzable in spatial terms—with the repulsive social-political ideas of a few (or one) of the Anglo-American writers of the post-World War I generation. Kermode has remarked, in a letter released for publication, that he believes the theory of spatial form to be now merely a relic of the past, "an outmoded period aesthetic."[16] This may very well be true; critical theories date very rapidly, especially in our time of a frantic quest for novelty in the arts. More relevant, though, is that Frank Kermode himself cannot view this idea *except* in such period terms, exclusively in relation to his own experiences and those of his generation in the Second World War. All this is perfectly human and perfectly comprehensible; but it does indicate an unwillingness to move beyond a fixed point, to evolve, and to develop a less traumatized perspective. In any case, it scarcely justifies a condemnation of spatial form as a theory that no longer has any connection with the literature of the present. On the contrary, the very forcefulness of Kermode's attack would seem to indicate that the theory is far from moribund; and when he quotes Robbe-Grillet to the effect that, in the *nouveau roman*, "le temps se trouve coupé de sa temporalité," he may well have suspected that spatial form is alive and well and very much at home in Paris.[17]

Such considerations should help to explain why Kermode reacts so vehemently, and so illogically, to any possibility that his own ideas might be thought to resemble a theory of spatial form. They also help to clarify why, though he is so close and careful a reader of Spenser, Shakespeare, Sartre, Yeats, Wallace Stevens et al., he seems incapable of referring to my article without falling into some error or misapprehension. In his view, I "implied that although books are inescapably of the element of time, their formal organization is to be apprehended as spatial; one would read them twice, as it were, once for time and once for space." In fact, however, I advanced no such general thesis. What I said was that *certain* works of twentieth-century literature, because of their experiments with language and narrative structure, required a reader to approach them as a spatial configuration rather than as a temporal continuum. Even though I should now agree that *all* works of literature contain elements of spatiality, I would still maintain that to view them in spatial terms becomes critically significant only when this aspect of their structure asserts a certain dominance.

Again, speaking of *Ulysses*, Kermode says rightly that it is full of contingency; hence, he thinks it unlikely that, as I claimed, Joyce believed "a unified spatial apprehension of his work would ultimately be possible." Presumably to refute me, he cites Arnold Goldman, who remarked that, since *Ulysses* is full of nonsignificant coincidences, "we are forced to carry ultimate explanations to the novel's end." But this is precisely what I say myself, more elliptically, in the oft-quoted assertion that *Ulysses* could not be read but only re-read; the unified spatial apprehension *cannot* occur on a first reading, though Joyce postulated it as the basis of his formal structure. So far as Proust is concerned, Kermode remarks that Marcel, in the recognition scene, "is not talking about spatial form" (whoever said he was?), and that "the experiences reserved for permanent meaning, carried out of the flux of time, surely do not make a pattern in space." Just what Kermode means here by a "pattern in space" is very far from being clear; but so far as it implies anything like spatial extension, it entirely misses the point. To clarify the issue, let me cite a passage from Proust not contained in my original text, and which I came across only on a recent re-reading.

When Albertine played the pianola for Marcel, she usually chose rolls that he had already heard two or three times, knowing that such repetition gave him a particular pleasure. Why was this so? "She divined," he explains, "that at the third or fourth hearing, my intelligence, in having grasped, and consequently placed at the same distance, all the parts, no longer having to exert any activity with respect to them, had reciprocally stretched and immobilized them on a uniform level." In other words, no longer required to follow the course of their unrolling in time, Marcel's intelligence placed the various parts together so that their relation could be grasped as a simultaneity. This passage prefigures the recognition scene, in which a very similar process takes place in relation to the temporality of people's lives, and where, as I wrote, "by the discontinuous presentation of character Proust forces *the reader* to juxtapose disparate images [of his characters] spatially, *in a moment of time,* so that the experience of time's passage is communicated directly to [the reader's] sensibility" (italics added). This has nothing to do with a "pattern in space," but everything with the reader's perception of the identity of the past and present images of the same characters "in a moment of time, that is to say, space."

Whether Frank Kermode has read me rightly or wrongly is hardly a matter of earthshaking consequence;

and I should not have wearied the reader with the above explanations if I were not persuaded that a more important issue is involved. I wished to show that there are no *substantive* grounds for the quarrel that Kermode has chosen to pick with my ideas, not for the puerile motive of self-vindication, but because I think it crucial to sweep away the obfuscation that this supposed disagreement tends to create. Actually, as I stated at the beginning of this discussion, it seems to me that Kermode has *accepted* the substance of my ideas (call them by whatever name you please), while pretending to be their most determined antagonist. And in fact, as I have suggested already, we have both developed different parts of the same theory.

My own contribution relates to twentieth-century literature, where spatialization enters so fundamentally into the very structure of language and the organization of narrative units that, as Kermode is forced to concede, "Frank says quite rightly that a good deal of modern literature is designed to be apprehended thus." He deals with the literature of the past, where spatialization (or, as he calls it, *plot-concordance*) was still a tendency that had by no means yet emerged in as radical a manner as in modernity. Both may be seen, and should be seen, as part of a unified theory, which has the inestimable advantage of linking experimental modernism with the past in an unbroken continuity. Moreover, such a theory allows us to view the present, not as a break, but rather as a limit-case, an intensification and accentuation of potentialities present in literature almost from the start. One of Kermode's essential aims in *The Sense of an Ending* was precisely to argue in favor of continuity and to reject the schismatic notion that a clean break with the past was either desirable or possible. It seems to me that he succeeded better than he knew, and that in polemicizing with spatial form he merely perpetuates a schism which the deeper thrust of his own ideas has done much to reveal as nugatory and obsolete.

What is necessary for the future, in my view, is to recognize that we now have the basis for a unified theory of literary structures and to work to fill in the outlines already sketched. Indeed, Kermode's extremely suggestive ideas about the relation of such structures to the religious and apocalyptic imagination pave the way for fruitful historical correlations between certain types of structure and certain kinds of collective imaginative experiences. Can we work out any sort of relations between the two in more detail? Why should the picaresque plot have dominated the novel for so long? Why should the much tighter Gothic structure have taken over in the late eighteenth century? These are some of the questions that immediately suggest themselves, and which Kermode has opened up for further exploration. It is because his ideas on this score seem to me so promising that I have taken all this trouble to exorcise the needless argument between us and to clear the way for the possibility of genuine progress toward a theory of literature grounded both in cultural psychology and in history.

Postscript

In his reply to the initial publication of this essay in Critical Inquiry, *Kermode continued to insist that modernism as an international phenomenon "was powerfully associated with the extreme Right and that there is "overwhelming evidence to prove this true." If it is not true, he candidly admits, "my whole position would be much weakened."* [18] *So far as this asserts that modernism tends to be more associated with the*

Right than with the Left in the broad sense (we are not talking about official communism), then I equally insist that it is not true and that Kermode's position is very weak indeed.

To buttress his case, Kermode offers a quotation from Renato Poggioli which counters the assumption that "aesthetic radicalism, revolutionaries in art and revolutionaries in politics" automatically or even predominantly go hand in hand.[19] *This is of course not true; but neither is the opposite—namely, Kermode's position that modernism and fascism are linked together in some fundamental way. Since Kermode accepts Poggioli as competent to speak on the issue, let me offer another quotation from him: "We must deny the hypothesis that the relation between avant-garde art (or art generally) and politics can be established a priori. Such a connection can only be determined a posteriori, from the viewpoint of the avant-garde's own political opinions and convictions."*[20]

The question at issue, then, as Kermode rightly states, is "whether it was proper of [him] to assert a relationship between modernist spatialising and political and cultural fascism." What does Poggioli say on this point? "Actually . . . the only omnipresent or recurring political ideology within the avant-garde is the least political or the most antipolitical of all: libertarianism or anarchism."[21] *So that while it was perfectly proper for Kermode to assert his relationship for the English situation, this national connection does not, as he always tends to assume, have any general applicability or validity.*

Notes

1. "Spatial Form in Modern Literature," first published in *Sewanee Review* 53 (Spring, Summer, Autumn 1945); revised version in my *The Widening Gyre* (New Brunswick, N.J., 1963; reprinted Bloomington, Ind., 1968), 3–62.

2. Roger Shattuck, *Marcel Proust* (New York, 1974), 116; see also my review of Shattuck's *Proust's Binoculars* in *Partisan Review* 31, no. 1 (1964), 135–143.
3. Gérard Genette, *Figures* (Paris, 1966), 40.
4. G. Giovannini, "Method in the Study of Literature in Its Relation to the Other Fine Arts," *Journal of Aesthetics and Art Criticism* 8 (1950), 185–195.
5. Walter Sutton, "The Literary Image and the Reader," *Journal of Aesthetics and Art Criticism* 16 (1957), 112–123.
6. Quoted by Monroe K. Spears, in *Dionysius and the City* (New York, 1970), 80, italics added.
7. Erich Auerbach, "Figura," *Scenes from the Drama of European Literature* (New York, 1959), 11–76. Shortly after making the above comparison between the techniques of modernism and Auerbach's conception of "figura," I came across the following passage in Julio Cortázar's brilliant experimental novel, *Hopscotch* (trans. Gregory Rabassa [New York, 1975], 488–489). It is contained in the reflections of a novelist Morelli, obviously Cortázar's artistic *alter ego* and who serves as commentator. (Italics in text.)

> To accustom one's self to use the expression *figure* instead of *image*, to avoid confusions. Yes, everything coincides. But it is not a question of return to the Middle Ages or anything like it. The mistake of postulating an absolute historical time; there are different times even though they may also be parallel. In this sense, one of the times of the so-called Middle Ages can coincide with one of the times of the Modern Ages. And that time is what has been perceived and inhabited by painters and writers who refuse to seek support in what surrounds them, to be "modern" in the

sense that their contemporaries understand them, which does not mean that they choose to be anachronistic; they are simply on the margin of the superficial time of their period, and from that other time where everything conforms to the condition of *figure*, where everything has value as a sign and not as a theme of description, they attempt a work which may seem alien or antagonistic to the time and history surrounding them, and which nonetheless includes it, explains it, and in the last analysis orients it towards a transcendence within whose limits man is waiting.

8. Sergei Eisenstein, *Film Form and Film Sense* (New York, 1957), 3–7. This edition consists of two books paginated separately; the reference is to the second volume, *Film Sense*.

9. Alain Robbe-Grillet, *Pour un nouveau roman* (Paris, 1963), 164.

10. Ernst Cassirer, *The Philosophy of Symbolic Forms*, 3 vols., trans. Ralph Manheim (New Haven, Conn., 1953–1957), 2:96.

11. Philip Rahv, "The Myth and the Powerhouse," *Literature and the Sixth Sense* (Boston, 1969), 202–215.

12. An extremely sophisticated Marxist treatment of the problems of modernism in the plastic arts, which touches on the same theoretical questions as in literature, may be found in R. Bianchi Bandinelli, *Organicità e astrazione* (Milan, 1956). The author was professor of archaeology and Greek and Roman art at the University of Florence, an eminent scholar, and an important member of the Italian Communist party. Professor Bianchi Bandinelli's brochure, which contains some extremely interesting passages on regression in art, refers to Worringer only in pass-

ing and does not mention *Abstraction and Empathy;* but he sees abstraction in modern art in exactly the terms that Worringer defined. Refusing to condemn it outright ("*non si tratta, dunque, di pronunziare un condanna*"), he considers it as the inevitable product of the sickness of capitalist culture, doomed to disappear and be replaced by humanism once its contradictions have been resolved in the new communist society.

13. Frank Kermode, *Wallace Stevens* (London, 1961).
14. For the sake of the record, and in view of the unpleasant insinuation contained in the quoted phrase, I should like to cite a passage from my article on Thomas Mann's *Dr. Faustus,* which originally appeared in a review of the book published in 1949.

> It is hardly possible any longer to overlook the union in modern art of the most daring intellectual and aesthetic modernity with a rejection of humanism and liberalism and a preference—both formally and ideologically—for the primitive, the mythical, and the irrational. To be sure, this has not necessarily resulted in an alliance with the forces of political retrogression; nor did it do so, we should remember, in the case of Leverkuhn himself, whose music was considered *Kulturbolschewismus* by the masters of the Third Reich. Still, the careers of Knut Hamsum, Ezra Pound, and Drieu la Rochelle; the political pronouncements of Yeats, Eliot (in the mid-thirties), Wyndham Lewis, and Gottfried Benn; the proto-Fascist tendencies in the work of D. H. Lawrence and Stefan George—all this reveals to what extent Thomas Mann has managed to raise to the level of sovereign art the problematic nature of modern culture itself. As modern life has become more and more

rationalized, mechanized, and industrialized, art has been driven into a more and more frenzied and violent assault on a world in which the total dimension of the spirit has been reduced to a stifling materialistic utilitarianism. The legitimacy and necessity of such a revolt is beyond question; yet its danger is no less evident. For it is an uncomfortable but inescapable truth that, if some of our noblest artistic expressions were to be translated tomorrow into practical, political terms, the result would only be to play into the hands of some form of tyranny and oppression. (*The Widening Gyre*, 158–159)

Kermode would do well to take to heart the lesson of *Dr. Faustus*, which dramatizes so majestically the very center of his own preoccupations. And Mann should teach him not to make such facile identifications between Fascism and avant-garde art, while recognizing how closely they can sometimes become allied in spirit. In fact, however, no totalitarian regime has ever tolerated the avant-garde after taking power, whatever the overt politics of the artists concerned, or whether the regime used the slogans of the right or the left.

15. Octavio Paz, *Children of the Mire*, trans. Rachel Phillips (Cambridge, Mass., 1974), 109–110.

16. The letter is cited in Ronald E. Foust, *The Place of Spatial Form in Modern Criticism* (Ph.D. diss., University of Maryland, 1975), 216. I assume that Professor Foust would not have used this personal letter unless he had received permission to do so from the writer.

17. It is not without significance that the article was considered still interesting enough to be translated,

in part, into French in 1972: "La forme spatiale dans la litterature moderne." *Poetique* 10 (1972), 244–266.

18. Frank Kermode, "A Reply to Joseph Frank," *Critical Inquiry* 4 (1978), 579–588.

19. Renato Poggioli, *The Theory of the Avant-Garde,* trans. Gerald Fitzgerald (New York, 1971), 95.

20. Ibid., 95.

21. Ibid., 97.

3

*S*patial Form: Some Further Reflections

I n "Spatial Form: An Answer to Critics," I defended myself vigorously—and, I hope, effectively—against what seemed to me incomprehension and unjustified cultural-political antagonism; but it should not be imagined that I think my ideas on spatial form immune to criticism. Far from it; and if I were writing my essay today, I should certainly make one important change. The necessity for such a revision was brought home to me by a pertinent comment contained in Hans Meyerhoff's excellent book *Time in Literature*. Meyerhoff picks up my term *symbolic reference* and also cites my remark that Joyce attempted to create in *Ulysses* "the impression of simultaneity for the life of a whole teeming city"; but he criticizes me for "failing to recognize the importance of the distinction between physical and psychological time" and for not discussing "the correlation between the structure of psychological time and the structure of the self."[1] Both of these criticisms are very relevant, and they point to a weakness in my essay that may be traced back to a single source.

This source, as I now realize, is the accidental circumstance that my work took its origin in a preoccupation with *Nightwood*. While unquestionably a work of remarkable literary quality, *Nightwood* was not destined, as the passage of time has shown, to exercise a major influence on the course of the novel;[2] quite the contrary, its metaphoric texture, which transforms the world into "soliloquists' images,"[3] has remained something of a sport, technically speaking. Much more influential have been the efforts of stream-of-consciousness writers such as Joyce, Faulkner, and Virginia Woolf to break up language itself so that it would reproduce the movements of consciousness either on the reflexive or prereflexive level. This effort to depict consciousness is what dramatizes the difference between physical and psychological time, and also calls into question the unity of the self. Despite my remarks on Joyce and Proust, I did not pay sufficient attention to these issues because neither arose in relation to *Nightwood*. Hence what I now consider a rather unbalanced perspective in my essay—not so much because of the amount of space devoted to *Nightwood*, but rather because of the neglect of the main line of novelistic development in which spatial form appears in its sharpest contours and with the richest philosophical-cultural implications.

Wylie Sypher has pointed out that "the loss of the self" is one of the dominant tendencies of both modernism and postmodernism;[4] and such loss is of course another symptom of what I called "the transmutation of the time-world of history into the timeless world of myth." The self no longer feels itself to be an active, individual force operating in the real world of history and time; it exists, if at all, only through its assimilation into a mythical world of eternal prototypes. I remarked upon this tendency in the concluding pages of my essay, but could have discussed it more effectively in the context of the dissolution of the self in stream-of-consciousness fiction.

Even though this modification is the only major change that, with the benefit of hindsight, I should wish to have made in my original text, this does not mean that I think my essay exhausts the discussion of the problem. Quite the contrary, it merely initiates a continuing exploration of a question whose larger implications have only recently begun to become clear. The developments in literary criticism in recent years have created a new context within which the idea of spatial form can now be situated and whose effect has been greatly to extend the range and applicability of the concept as I first propounded it. This context has arisen from the fusion of anthropology, information theory, structural linguistics, and literary criticism that began with the Russian Formalists, was carried on in the Prague Linguistic circle, and now goes by the name of French Structuralism. The theories of this critical movement have shown that spatial form is not only a concept relevant to a particular phenomenon of avant-garde writing but that it plays a role, even if only a subordinate one, throughout the entire history of literature. The radical nature of the experiments of literary modernism brought spatial form to the foreground of critical consciousness; but now that the novelty has worn off, it has become possible to locate the concept in relation to a much wider literary horizon. Spatial form, so far as I can judge, is at present in the process of being assimilated into a much more general theory of the literary text; and I should like to conclude these reconsiderations with some remarks on the ways this is being done.

. . .

The development of this general theory is obviously occurring (or has already occurred, to a large extent) with regard to poetry, largely as a result of the growing influence of the theories of Roman Jakobson. My own views were worked out without a knowledge of Jakobson's articles; but Lessing and modern literature had led me to similar conclusions, even though I was not able to express them with the precision that Jakobson could command as a professional linguist. It may seem surprising, at first sight, that such a similarity of views should have emerged by chance; but a little reflection shows that Jakobson's ideas and my own had numerous points of contact (even if not personal ones). Jakobson, after all, formed his ideas in the atmosphere of Russian Futurism and, as a young man, was a personal friend both of Khlebnikov and Mayakovsky. The ideas about poetry circulating in the pre-revolutionary Russia of his youth had many similarities with those that influenced Eliot, Pound, and the Anglo-Americans: both drew from the common source of French Symbolist aesthetics.[5] Hence, even though I had available only Anglo-American criticism and French literary criticism of the 1920s and '30s (the latter now much underestimated in its own country), both Jakobson and I were working in the same cultural climate. And one should remember, in any case, that experimental modernism is a world-wide movement whose formal features remain quite similar across national boundaries.[6]

Jakobson's views are thus rooted in his own experience of poetic modernism, but they take their systematic point of departure from Saussure's theory of language. Saussure had no connection, so far as I am aware, with the avant-garde (Symbolist) literature of his own day; yet if someone had wished to design a theory of language adapted to rationalize modernist poetry, he could not have done better than this retiring and socially conservative scion of the Genevan aristocracy. For Saussure defines the sign not as the linkage of a name with a thing but rather of a *sound-image* with a concept; in other words, language is now seen as a self-enclosed system of sound-images and concepts. *Meaning* is defined in terms of the differential relations within the system, not in terms of the relation of the sign to a reality external to language itself. It is not difficult to see how such a view of language harmonizes with that of modern poetry, where referentiality is relegated to a secondary position, or disregarded entirely, and the internal relations of words to each other play a predominant role. Jakobson saw this relationship and used it as the basis of his theory of poetic language; and though I did not have Saussure's theories at my disposal, what I said about the *space-logic* of modern poetry is quite similar. "The primary reference of any word-group [in a modernist poem]," I wrote, "is to something inside the poem itself," that is, the system of self-reflexive signs that constitute the text. And I added that the space-logic of such self-reflexiveness "demands a complete reorientation in the reader's attitude toward language." Actually, as I now know, such a reorientation had already taken place in linguistics under Saussure's influence; and the impact of Jakobson's work, both in linguistics and literary criticism, has led to a general acceptance of that reorientation as part of modern literary awareness.

Jakobson's now classic definition of poetic language in terms of information theory, contained in his article "Linguistics and Poetics,"[7] incorporates this space-logic of modern poetry into a much wider framework; but such space-logic, all the same, receives the place of honor by being assigned the function of a universal poetic signifier. There are, Jakobson says, six factors involved in the sending and receiving of any message: sender, message, receiver, context, contact (the physical or psychological medium), code. Each of these factors gives rise to a different linguistic function; and though all are contained in any message, one or another, in any particular case, may have greater dominance in the hierarchy of functions. A poetic message is distinguished by the dominance of the *message itself*, in preference, for example, to the dominance of the (extralinguistic) context. I had called the same phenomenon "the principle of reflexive reference" in modern poetry. In a poetic message, Jakobson explains further, *"the poetic function projects the principle of equivalence from the axis of selection into the axis of combination"* (italics in original). What this means is that the organization of words in the poem ("the axis of combination") is no longer controlled, as in ordinary language, exclusively by the syntactical order of whatever language is being used; the latter is counterbalanced by the "principle of equivalence" between words, based on their inner relations of similarity or dissimilarity, synonymy or antinomy, which governs "the axis of selection." Such a "principle of equivalence" usually determines the *choice* of words in any ordinary message but not their combination in a sequence. In a poetic message, then, the customary order of combination is overlaid by an order based on "equivalence"— that is, by a space-logic which runs counter to the linear temporality of syntactical structure.

Jakobson's analysis of Baudelaire's "Les Chats," written in collaboration with Lévi-Strauss, is an attempt to demonstrate the dense network of linguistic "equivalences" that underlie the poem and are integrated with its syntactical construction. Such application of Jakobson's views to particular poems has excited a great deal of controversy, and his readings, it has now become clear, are very vulnerable in detail. The trouble seems to be that, in interpreting the poetry of the past, Jakobson tends to approach it *as if* it were already modern—as if the purely grammatical and linguistic structures of "equivalence" dominated totally the semantic level.[8] This is of course far from being the case; but he has nonetheless succeeded in demonstrating the existence of supporting and quite complex structures of such "equivalence" in poems that are hardly at all "difficult" in the modern sense. Jakobson has thus made a fundamental contribution to the study of poetic language, which proves that there is a space-logic of greater or lesser degree in all poetry. The point at which such space-logic becomes completely dominant—the point at which it breaks loose and radically reorders the sequential order of syntax—is the point at which "modernism" begins.

. . .

It was, however, not so much with regard to poetry as to the novel that the notion of spatial form made its greatest impact. For it focused attention on the opposition between the temporal nature of the narrative medium (language) and the experiments of such novelists as Joyce, Proust, and Djuna Barnes, who broke up narrative continuity in order to portray either the prereflexive stream of consciousness or the interweaving time-shifts of memory, or who composed in terms of symbolic imagery. Systematic experiments with point of view and time-shift had of course begun much earlier with James, Conrad, and Ford, not to mention the occasional sporadic anticipations of Sterne and Diderot. But it was only in the works of the great modernists, soon followed by Faulkner, Dos Passos, and a whole host of others (recent examples are the French *nouveau roman* and the Latin-American *nueva novela*), that the break with narrative sequence first became a significant aesthetic phenomenon.

Lessing proved immensely helpful and suggestive in

providing me with a way of grasping this evolution of form in narrative. For while I was not at all concerned with his particular problem—the rivalry between poetry and painting as imitative media—his emphasis on language as a linear-temporal structure gave me an insight into the dominant formal peculiarity of the avant-garde novel. Not that novelists were trying to portray "space" in any literal sense; but their experiments led them in a direction counter to the physical-perceptual nature of their medium. Lessing had advised poets to prefer action to description, and not to dwell on picturesque details, because action harmonized better with the linear-temporal character of language. Of course, he said nothing about the novel of his own time (though he was a great admirer of Sterne); and, in taking Homer as a standard, he was implicitly equating literature with oral recitation (he speaks in several places of the difference between literature and painting as being that between the ear and the eye). But Lessing's observations, all the same, did focus attention on the relation between the properties of language and the structure of narrative, and this helped me to define with more or less precision what had been happening in the modern novel. If, as Lessing did, one assumed as a norm that artists should shape their material to the requirements of their physical-perceptual medium, it was clear that the avant-garde novel was overtly defying any such norm and, indeed, going in quite the opposite direction.

This is where I stopped at the time, without asking myself any more questions and without worrying about the possible relations of these new developments to the past. In recent years, however, renewed attention has been focused on the problem I broached in the 1940s and which Lessing had broached much earlier: the relation of language to literary structure. Such attention has been prompted partly by the intensive researches of linguistic theory into the syntagmatic and paradigmatic properties of language and also by the animated discussion provoked by the experiments of the *nouveau roman*. In addition, the early work of the Russian Formalists has now become accessible in European languages, and their attempt to establish a poetics of prose forms in the 1920s anticipated many of the more current concerns. All this has created the basis of a more general theory of spatial form in narrative that is gradually beginning to emerge.

. . .

Of fundamental importance is the distinction drawn by the Formalists between *story* and *plot*. The first term refers to the events of a narrative arranged in the strict sequence of a causal-chronological order; the second, to the structure of these same events as they actually appear in any particular work. It was Victor Shklovsky who first stressed the importance of this distinction, and he did so in an essay on *Tristram Shandy*, which, as he explains, he wrote with the aim of seeing whether he could read this novel as he would a Futurist poem.[9] In other words, it was the obvious abandonment of syntactical sequence in modern poetry that first drew Shklovsky's attention, just as it had my own, to the possibility of a similar variety of form in the novel.

A bit later, basing his work on Shklovsky's, Boris Tomashevsky drew a related but broader distinction between what he called *bound motifs* and *free motifs* in any prose text. The first are essential to the causal-chronological sequence and cannot be eliminated without destroying the text entirely; the second are relatively independent of such sequence and can be combined in any order the writer desires. Such free motifs, Toma- shevsky remarks, "are presented so that the tale may be told artistically." In this perspective, *art* may be provi- sionally defined as the extent to which free motifs diver- sify the constraints of the bound motifs.[10] For, as Tzvetan Todorov has pointed out, causality and chronology dominate in nonliterary types of prose: "pure causality sends us back to practical discourse, pure temporality to the elementary forms of history (science)."[11] Hence it would appear that the "literariness" of a narrative work, its specific *artistic* quality, may be defined as the disjunc- tion between story and plot, that is, the manner in which the writer manipulates and distorts causal- chronological sequence; this would be analogous to the function Jakobson assigns to the "equivalences" as sig- nifiers of poetic language. And it would also follow that every narrative work of art necessarily includes ele- ments that may be called spatial since the relations of significance between such elements must be construed across gaps in the strict causal-chronological order of the text.

It is obvious that the closer the structure of a narrative conforms to causal-chronological sequence, the closer it corresponds to the linear-temporal order of language. It is now equally obvious, however, that such correspon- dence is contrary to the nature of narrative as an art form. Indeed, it is clear that all through the history of the novel a tension has existed between the linear-temporal nature of its medium (language) and the spatial elements re- quired by its nature as a work of art. Most of what are known as the "formal conventions" of the novel are an implicit agreement between writer and reader not to pay attention to this disjunction and to overlook the extent to which it exists. Shklovsky provocatively called *Tristram Shandy* the most "typical" novel in world literature (of course, it is one of the most *untypical*) because it "laid bare" all the conventions employed by the form, whose nature *as* conventions had become imperceptible through long familiarity.

For example, we do not feel jolted when, at the end of a chapter in a conventional novel, the author asks us to shift our attention to events in a parallel plot line that have been occurring simultaneously with those we have just read about. But we *do* feel jolted when Tristram Shandy, depicting his mother listening at a door, freezes that particular scene for ten-odd pages to follow another train of thought and then picks up the scene again when he is done. Nor does the average reader feel disturbed when, having come across a reference or allusion to a character early in a text, the physical appearance of the personage is delayed until a later stage. But it *does* seem odd that Tristram Shandy is not physically born until about two hundred pages of the novel devoted to his life have already been covered. Sterne, in other words, parodies the conventions by breaking into the continuity of sequences at eccentric points and also by highlighting through exaggeration the anomalies involved in reshaping causal-chronological sequence to serve the purposes of art.

The importance of this Russian Formalist contribution is that it focused attention, for the first time, on the existence of elements of spatial form (though the Formalists themselves never used such a term) in *all* narrative. In the opinion of Todorov, who has improved and updated Tomashevsky in his excellent survey of contemporary poetics, the Formalists were, however, approaching an idea of spatial form. Tomashevsky had noted that texts could be organized in two ways: either "causal-temporal relationships exist between thematic elements"; or, "the thematic elements are contemporaneous" and/or "there is some shift of theme without internal exposition of the causal connections." Citing this passage, Todorov calls the first type of structure "the logical-temporal order"; while "the second—which Tomashevsky identifies negatively—[is] the spatial order." [12] Spatial form is thus recognized as one of the permanent possibilities for the organization of all literary texts.

From this point of view, the emergence of spatial form in twentieth-century narrative should no longer be regarded as a radical break with tradition. Rather, it represents only what Jakobson would call a shift in the internal hierarchy of the elements composing a narrative structure. Predominant in the past were the bound motifs of causal-chronological sequence that, in conformity with the original oral nature of narrative, ruled over the free motifs and kept them under strict control (with a few exceptions, considered abnormal, like *Tristram Shandy* and *Jacques le fataliste*). But, beginning with the second half of the nineteenth century, this predominance of causal-chronological sequence came to be seriously weakened. And the most radical proponents of the *nouveau roman*—such as Philippe Sollers and the *Tel Quel* group, who some years back saw *Finnegans Wake* as the norm of narrative in the future—hope now to wipe out all traces of causal-chronological sequence once and for all. Like all such extremes, however, this ambition is likely to remain as peripheral a phenomenon as concrete poetry. Such is my opinion, for the reasons wryly given by Horacio Oliveira in Julio Cortázar's *Hopscotch* when he is asked to define "the absolute." It is, he says, "just that moment in which something attains its maximum depth, its maximum reach, its maximum sense, and becomes completely uninteresting."[13] Quite so, and Sollers has now (1990) returned to the narrative middle ground.

Todorov notes that the spatial order of literary works has been studied primarily in poetry, and he refers to the writings of Jakobson as the most systematic effort made in this direction. Narrative spatial form is still a relatively unexplored domain, despite the fact that, as he points out, "today, literature is turning towards narratives of a spatial and temporal type, to the detriment of causality" (by "temporal" Todorov means "le temps de l'écriture," that is, the reflexive temporality of the literary act itself, not narrative temporality in the old sense).[14] There is thus much to be done in working out the particular modalities of spatial form in narrative as it continues to evolve as well as in defining its relations to the literary tradition. On a theoretical level, I admire the work done in this direction by Gérard Genette, who, along with Todorov, has in my view made the most interesting suggestions toward what can become the basis of an enlarged theory of narrative spatial form.

• • •

It is Genette who has seen most clearly the theoretical implications of the *nouveau roman* and has developed them in the context of a sweeping view of the history of narrative as a whole. It is instructive to note how he returns inevitably to Lessing's old problem (though without specific reference to his predecessor) and carries it forward in the light of the contemporary situation. Discussing the relation between narration and description in his brilliant article "Frontières du récit," he writes:

> Narration attaches itself to actions and events considered as pure processes, and thus it puts the emphasis on the temporal and dramatic aspect of *récit;* description on the contrary, because it lingers on objects and things considered in their simultaneity, and because it envisages processes themselves as spectacles, seems to suspend the course of time and contributes to spread the *récit* in space.[15]

This is of course Lessing restated—except that the use of description is no longer seen as an attempt to compete with the effect of painting, and it is now treated as an indigenous component of narrative.

Nonetheless, just as Lessing did, Genette notes an inherent imbalance in the relation of these two narrative components (narration and description) to language.

> The most significant difference between them would perhaps be that narration restores, in the temporal succession of its discourse, the equally temporal succession of events, while description has to model in successiveness the representation of objects coexisting and juxtaposed in space; narrative language would thus be distinguished by a sort of temporal coincidence with its object, while descriptive language, on the contrary, would be irreparably deprived of such coincidence.[16]

But this no longer means that description should be totally subordinate to narration, as Lessing had argued; "this opposition," Genette maintains, "loses much of its force in written literature [visual rather than oral], where nothing prevents the reader from retracing his steps and considering the text, in its simultaneous spatiality, as an *analogon* of the spectacle it describes; the *calligrammes* of Apollinaire or the graphic dispositions of a *Coup de dés* only push to the limit the exploitation of certain latent resources of written expression." [17] Such remarks, as I see them, go a long way to establish the theory of spatial form in our modern awareness of the synchronic dimensions of language in a written text; and this awareness is now regarded merely as the extension of a traditional narrative component. Indeed if, as I should like to suggest, one enlarges Genette's terms to think of description as including the internal world of the psyche as well as the external world of nature and society, the attempt to convey simultaneity by abrupt time-shifts and the use of stream of consciousness may well be considered part of description in this amplified sense.

Genette also makes some extremely interesting historical observations on the varying role of these two narrative components. In the classical tradition, the function of description was ornamental and decorative; and Lessing reacted against the excess of such ornamentation as part of his campaign against French Neoclassicism (Boileau, on the other hand, counseled writers of epics "*Soyez riche et pompeux dans vos descriptions*"). It was the excess of such ornamentation in the Baroque period, as Genette observes, that "ended by destroying the equilibrium of the narrative poem in its decline." But, at the beginning of the nineteenth century, description reached a new synthesis with narration in the novel. Far from receding into the background, description took on a new importance in Balzac because its function became explicative and symbolic, no longer merely decorative. "The physical portraits, the descriptions of clothes and furniture, tend, in Balzac and his realist successors, to reveal and, at the same time, to justify the psychology of the characters, of which they are at once the sign, the cause, and the effect. Description becomes here what it never was in the classical period, a major element of the exposition."[18] (Such a use of description, we may note in passing, actually began in the Gothic novel and reached Balzac by way of Scott and the historical novel.)

Genette points out, however, that the more recent evolution of the novel has seen what appears to be the increasing liberation of description from its subordination to narration, though he is not sure that it should be interpreted in this way. "The work of Robbe-Grillet," he writes,

> appears perhaps more as an effort to construct a *récit* (an *histoire*) through the exclusive means of descriptions imperceptibly modified from page to page, which may be seen, at one and the same time, as a spectacular promotion of the descriptive function and a striking confirmation of its irreducible subordination to narration.[19]

Whether one can still speak of description as *subordinate* in a work composed exclusively of the variation of descriptive fragments seems very doubtful; but this minor point does not detract from the usefulness of Genette's categories.[20] For their value is that they help us to view the history of spatial form in terms of the changing relationships between description and narration.

Another section of the same essay offers an additional vantage point from which to survey the same problem.

Using some linguistic observations of Émile Benveniste as his point of departure, Genette here shifts from the inner-textual interplay between narration and description to that of the relation between text and narrator. Benveniste distinguishes between what he calls *récit* and *discours* in terms of whether or not the presence of a locutor is grammatically indicated. *Récit* tends to eliminate any such reference, whether explicit or implied; *discours* brings the personal source of utterance to the foreground, or at least does not try to conceal such a presence. *Récit* is the pure form of objective narration; *discours* the pure form of subjective narration; neither, however, is ever found in a pure state, and they "contaminate" each other all through the history of narrative. But here again, all the same, there is another imbalance: Genette maintains that *discours* is the widest and most universal category of linguistic expression and can easily contain and include passages of *récit* without strain. *Récit*, on the other hand, "is a particular mode, *set apart*, defined by a certain number of exclusions and restrictive conditions (avoidance of the present, of the first person, etc.)."[21] As a result, *récit* is, comparatively, a more artificial and limited form; even though it cannot avoid including *discours*, when it does so its norms always appear violated.

Récit, obviously, aims so far as possible at being the pure form of causal-chronological sequence; but it is constantly being interfered with by *discours*, which calls attention away from the flow of events to the narrator and the process of narration. Genette analyzes this phenomenon without relating it to the issues that he raised when speaking of narration and description; but the two points of view are obviously connected. For just as description tends to spatialize narration, so *discours* inevitably exercises a more or less perceptible spatializing effect, on the micro-narrative level, by its constant interruption of the rhythm of pure chronicity. This helps to explain why an increase of interest in man's subjective and emotional life, when translated into terms of literary form, automatically seems to lead to an increase in the spatialization of narrative (sentimentalism in the mid-eighteenth century, the period of the epistolary novel and Sterne, and the influence of Freud and Bergson at the beginning of the twentieth). *Récit,* according to Genette, celebrated its greatest triumphs in the nineteenth-century novel with Balzac and Tolstoy; but it has now been almost entirely replaced by *discours* in the avant-garde novel of the 1920s and its continuator in French literature, the *nouveau roman.* Proust is of course the obvious exemplar (curiously he is not mentioned in this context), but Genette does refer to Joyce and Faulkner as writers who transfer the *récit* "to the interior *discours* of their principal characters." In the *nouveau roman,* the tendency is "to absorb the *récit* into the present *discours* of the writer in the course of writing."[22] The increasing spatialization of the novel, as we see, is clearly correlated with the growing preponderance of *discours;* and spatial form can thus be regarded as a function of the fluctuating historical relations between these two linguistic modes.

· · ·

Genette's *Figures III* contains a study of narrative structure, "Discours du récit," which seems to me the most substantial contribution to the poetics of the novel since Wayne Booth's, and of equally classic stature. This is not the place to discuss the work in detail; but a glance at the index reveals a large number of technical terms (*achronie, structure acronique, anachronie, anisocronie, isochronie analepse, prolepse*), all of which refer to various ways in which temporality and causal-chronological sequence are manipulated in a narrative text. The examples come mostly, though not exclusively, from Proust; and they constitute, so far as my knowledge goes, the most acute and systematic account of such structures ever attempted in criticism. What Genette has written is, for a good part, a study in spatial form; and students of the subject have a good deal to learn from his pages.

Even more, one of his other essays in *Figures II*, "La Littérature et l'espace," contains a masterly analysis of the broader horizon against which the idea of narrative spatial form must now be seen. Bergson, at the beginning of the century, had accused language of betraying reality by spatializing the temporality of consciousness; and linguistics for the past half-century has confirmed Bergson's ideas without sharing his hostility. "In distinguishing rigorously between the word and language-system," Genette writes,

> and in giving first place to the latter in the *play* of language—defined as a system of purely differential relations, in which each element is conditioned by the place it occupies in a general ensemble and by the vertical and horizontal relations that it maintains with related and neighboring elements—it is undeniable that Saussure and his continuators have brought to the foreground a mode of being of language that one must call spatial, although we are dealing here, as Blanchot has written, with a spatiality "whose originality cannot be grasped in terms either of geometrical space or the space of practical life."[23]

Nor is it only linguistics, one may add, which has contributed to focus such sharp attention on this spatial aspect of language. Genette says nothing about the work that has been done, primarily by English and American writers, in exploring oral literature and folk poetry and in speculating on the vast changes that have occurred in literary consciousness as a result of the transition from oral to written literature. One thinks here essentially of the work of Albert Lord, but also of such names as Marshall McLuhan and Walter J. Ong, who have stressed the wider cultural ramifications of this transition. The theories of such writers support Genette's remark that "this spatiality of language which commands and determines every act of speech, is in some way made manifest, placed in evidence, and moreover accentuated in a literary work by the use of a written text." [24]

Genette then goes on to outline, in broad strokes, the contemporary view of the literary work that has gradually evolved as a result of the increasing awareness of the crucial nature of this evolution from speech to writing.

> One has long considered writing, and particularly the writing called phonetic such as we conceive and utilize it, or believe we utilize it, in the West, as a simple means for the notation of speech. Today we are beginning to understand that it is a bit more than that. . . . Because of the specific spatiality to which we have referred, language (and thus thought) is already a kind of writing, or, if one prefers, the manifest spatiality of writing may be taken as a symbol for the profound spatiality of language. And, at the very least, for we who live in a civilization in which literature is identified with the written, this spatial mode of its existence cannot be considered accidental or negligible. Since Mallarmé, we have learned to recognize (to re-cognize) the so-called visual resources of script and of typo-

graphical arrangement; and of the existence of the Book as a kind of total object; and this change of perspective has made us more attentive to the spatiality of writing, to the atemporal disposition of signs, words, phrases, and discourse in the simultaneity of what is called a text. [25]

Finally, the result has been to change our notion of what it means to read.

It is not true that reading is only that continual unfolding accompanying the hours as they pass of which Proust spoke with reference to his boyhood; and the author of *La Recherche du temps perdu* no doubt knew this better than anyone—he who demanded of his reader an attention to what he called the "telescopic" character of his work, that is, to the relations at long distance established between episodes far removed from each other in the temporal continuity of a linear reading (but, it should be noted, singularly close in the written space, in the paginated thickness of the volume), and which requires for its consideration a sort of simultaneous perception of the total unity of the work, a unity which resides not solely in the horizontal relations of continuity and succession, but also in the relations that may be called vertical or transversal, those effects of expectation, of response, of symmetry, of perspective, which prompted Proust himself to compare his work to a cathedral. To read as it is necessary to read such works (are there any others?) is really to reread; it is already to have reread, to have traversed a book tirelessly in all directions, in all its dimensions. One may say, then, that the space of a book, like that of a page, is not passively subject to the time of a linear reading; so far as the book reveals and fulfills itself completely, it never stops diverting and reversing such a reading, and thus, in a sense, abolishes it.[26]

It is very gratifying for me to observe how many of these ideas echo my own of thirty years earlier (without any direct influence, as Genette has informed me in a letter), while developing them far beyond what would have been possible for me at that time.[27] And such convergence, as well as such continuity, seems to me to prove that the idea of spatial form in literature is much more than simply a provocative critical paradox (though it is also that as well). It is, I believe, a concept which satisfies the Hegelian requirement that ideas should grasp the inner movement of cultural reality itself.

Notes

1. Hans Meyerhoff. *Time in Literature* (Berkeley and Los Angeles, 1955), 152.
2. See Melvin J. Friedman, *Stream of Consciousness: A Study in Literary Method* (New Haven, Conn., 1955), 261–262.
3. Ralph Freedman, *The Lyrical Novel* (Princeton, N.J., 1963), 278.
4. Wylie Sypher, *Loss of the Self in Modern Literature and Art* (New York, 1964).
5. See the excellent discussion of Jakobson's relation to modern poetry in Tzvetan Todorov, *Théories du symbole* (Paris, 1977), 339–352.
6. In Russia, Khlebnikov, Mayakovsky, Pasternak, Biely; in England, Pound, Eliot, Joyce, Virginia Woolf; in France, Rimbaud, Mallarmé, Apollinaire, Proust, and now proponents of the *nouveau roman*.
7. Roman Jakobson, *Essais de linguistique générale* (Paris,

1963), 208–248. I refer to Jakobson's English essay in French because the latter version was more easily accessible to me at the time of writing. The original can now be found in Roman Jakobson, *Language in Literature*, ed. Krystyna Pomorska and Stephen Rudy (Cambridge, Mass., 1987). For a more extensive treatment of Jakobson, see my essay, "Roman Jakobson: The Master Linguist," in Joseph Frank, *Through the Russian Prism* (Princeton, N.J., 1990), 3–17.

8. As Gérard Genette has shown, Jakobson has constantly wavered in his attitude toward the relation of sound and significance in poetry. See "Formalisme et language poétique," *Comparative Literature* 28 (1976), 233–243.

9. Shklovsky's essay has been translated in *Russian Formalist Criticism*, trans. Lee T. Lemon and Marion J. Reis (Lincoln, Nebr., 1965), 25–57.

10. Tomashevsky's text is partially translated in *Russian Formalist Criticism*; see 68 for quotation.

11. Todorov, *Poétique* (Paris, 1973), 77; translations are my own.

12. Ibid., 68.

13. Julio Cortázar, *Hopscotch*, trans. Gregory Rabassa (New York, 1966), 47.

14. Todorov, 77.

15. Genette, *Figures II* (Paris, 1969), 59; translations are my own.

16. Ibid., 60.

17. Ibid.

18. Ibid., 59.

19. Ibid.

20. Genette, as it happened, read this essay and in a personal letter (Jan. 23, 1978) clarified the point about which I had expressed a reservation.

> I see that you reject the idea that even in Robbe-Grillet description is subordinate to narration. The formulation may well be surprising, and is probably not sufficiently explicated: I mean to say that the novels of R. G. (and this is why they are really novels), although they consist, so to speak, only of descriptions, all the same use these descriptions, more precisely their successive variations, indirectly to construct a narrative (*histoire*): that of the process of which these variations are the trace. In this sense, the descriptions perform, as much as those of Balzac though in a completely different manner, a narrative function to which they are subordinate, in the sense in which all means, no matter how abundant, are subordinate to their end, however discreet, or even dissimulated as the solutions of an enigma.

These words certainly help to elucidate his meaning, but perhaps the use of the term "subordination," which seems to imply some sort of overt and manifest dominance, will continue to give rise to misunderstanding.

21. Ibid., 66; italics in original.
22. Ibid., 67–68.
23. Ibid., 44–45.
24. Ibid., 45.
25. Ibid.
26. Ibid., 45–46.
27. In the letter already cited (note 20), Genette was also kind enough to write: "This text [the present essay] has confirmed for me the community of views that I noted in reading your *Spatial Form* in French translation (I did not know it before that date, and was unfortunately unable to take it into account in writing *Figures III*)."

4

André Malraux: A Metaphysics of Modern Art

T H E title of André Malraux's book, *The Psychology of Art*, is apt to prove misleading to prospective readers.[1] One could easily mistake the work for another of those elaborate treatises in so-called scientific psychology, whose laboratory experiments, at least when applied to the fine arts, have led to such distressingly meager and elementary results. Malraux, however, uses the term *psychology* in a much wider sense not customary in English. For him, the psychology of art is an attempt to define the general structure of the artistic response toward reality, and more particularly, toward the eternal human reality of destiny and death. Art, Malraux believes, is a mighty answer given by man to the menace of destiny; an answer flung back at fate by artists from the cave men to Picasso, but which has reached full self-consciousness only in modern art. Here, for the first time, the eternal metaphysical value of art is revealed in full clarity; and the purpose of Malraux's book, which should perhaps have been called a metaphysic rather than a psychology of art, is to exalt art's newly perceived status as "a re-creation of the universe in the face of Creation." In this respect, Malraux carries to an extreme point the tendency of modern culture to turn art into a secular religion—the religion of those for whom, as for Nietzsche, God is dead, but who cannot stop asking the questions that God once answered.

As French critics have noted, Malraux's *Psychology of Art* bears more than a slight resemblance to Nietzsche's *Birth of Tragedy*. Both books take their departure from some contemporary aesthetic phenomenon that seems to offer a new insight into the universal meaning of art (for Nietzsche this contemporary stimulus was Wagner's music drama, while for Malraux it is the aesthetic of Post-Impressionism); both are written with coruscating verbal brilliance and with a frenetic passion that scorns traditional historical categories as well as schoolroom concepts of orderly exposition; both are concerned with art, not primarily as a source of aesthetic pleasure but as a means of salvation. It is testimony to the stature of Malraux's work that it is not diminished by such a comparison; and the relation between the two books goes even deeper than the resemblances already noted. For Malraux, in some sense, may be said to be concerned with answering Nietzsche—or if not answering him, then attempting to counter some of the dangers released into Western culture by his thought. Whether or not Nietzsche intended to do so, his rapturous evocation of the irrational Dionysiac depths of Greek tragedy, his attack on Socratic reason as a cause of cultural aridity and stagnation, his celebration of the barbaric, the primitive, the sensual, and the ecstatic as sources of social-cultural fecundation and regeneration certainly helped to encourage the revaluation of these aspects of human life and to open the floodgates for the primacy they have since assumed in modern culture. Malraux, as it were, stands at the end of the development initiated by Nietzsche's first book. His own work may thus be seen as a last-ditch effort, by someone who has felt the full impact of Nietzsche's thought, to resurrect some of the values that Nietzsche's influence succeeded in placing in such deep discredit.

Aside from this general purpose, however, Malraux's

book should also be read for the wealth of concrete analyses of individual works, artists, and styles that it contains. Rarely, in modern writing on art, has such a wealth of expressive imagery been combined with so sure an insight into the historical and religious values embodied in particular art styles. One would have to go back to Ruskin and Walter Pater in English, or Taine and Hegel on the Continent, to find pages of comparable scope and grandeur. Whole sections of the book are prose poetry of a high order—but a poetry whose words are controlled, at every point, by a scrupulous precision in defining stylistic and historical nuances. This is not art history in the usual sense but in the grand style; and though art historians may carp, as the great Hellenist Wilamowitz did about Nietzsche, ordinary readers can only rejoice at the grandeur and the immense sweep of the perspectives opened on the most vital issues of our own cultural dilemmas. Malraux's book is not only a metaphysics of art but also an ethics of the history of culture; and as such its vision remains perennially relevant.

• • •

The first volume of Malraux's work, called "The Imaginary Museum," is a general introduction to his leading ideas on modern art, which are, in the second volume, extended to the history of art as a whole. By the title of this first volume, Malraux alludes symbolically to the process that, in his view, has led to a new understanding of the nature of art—an understanding based on a more extended knowledge of past art styles than has ever before been available. In perfecting the technical means of reproducing art works, modern man has created an "imaginary museum" for himself that places

him in a different relation to art than preceding generations. The growth of real museums from small private
collections had already, as Malraux points out, led to the
intellectualization of art, since in entering the museum
the art work was taken out of the spiritual context for
which it had been created and juxtaposed with other
works from dissimilar contexts, the only link between
them being their common quality as art. Whether originally created to glorify God as part of a cathedral or the
power of a ruling class as the portrait of a monarch, art
before the nineteenth century existed primarily by vir-
tue of its extra-aesthetic function; and the imaginary
museum of pictorial reproductions, which has now become the normal relation of modern man to art, shows
how far this loss of function has advanced. Yet at the
same time, by placing modern man in contact with the
totality of artistic expression—something that was possible only to a limited extent in the real museums of the
past—the true function of art as an autonomous human
activity has been brought into the foreground of aesthetic consciousness.

Up to the middle of the nineteenth century, this process took place in Europe within the framework of a unified aesthetic tradition. Speaking broadly, this tradition
was based, like Greek art, on a reconciliation of man
with nature and with God. It was under the impulse of
this reconciliation that European art, beginning in the
Renaissance, embarked on its quest to master the forms
of the natural world as they presented themselves to
commonsense perception. Art in the Renaissance, of
course, remained in the service of religion, as it had been
in the Middle Ages; but the Christianity of the Renaissance was no longer cleft by the tragic dualism between
the natural and the supernatural, between the sinful

world of the human and the awesome world of the divine, that had determined the stylistic distortions of natural forms in Romanesque and early Gothic art. "For the forms of a haunted world," Malraux writes, "those of a purgatory were substituted; of that Christianity which had shouldered so much anguish, soon nothing was to remain at Rome but a promise of Paradise. . . . The day when Nicholas of Cusa wrote 'Christ is the perfect man,' a Christian cycle closed at the same time as the Gates of Hell; the forms of Raphael could be born." For Giotto, in Malraux's view, painting a crucifix was an affirmation of the artist's religious faith; while for Leonardo, painting *The Last Supper* was no longer primarily an act of faith: it was the artistic embodiment of a "sublime tale." The task of the artist thus became to represent—in human terms, and in harmony with human vision—an ideal world of fiction. It became "less the painting of beautiful objects than that of imaginary objects which, if they became real, would be beautiful."

For several centuries, then, Italian art of the Renaissance continued in this direction, concentrating its efforts on mastering the representation of natural movement and using this mastery to express a harmonious world of fiction conceived in ideal human terms. But in the sixteenth century, the technical problems involved in depicting such a world had all been solved; and the result, as Malraux sees it, was a split between art as an expression of values in plastic terms and art as the representation of a particular subject matter—a split, in short, between style and representation. Up to this time the two had run parallel, for "every discovery in the expression of movements had been the consequence of a discovery of style," that is, of an expression of values through the plastic language of art. "Masaccio had not painted more 'true to life' than Giotto because he cared more about illusion, but because the place of man in the world that he knew how to incarnate was not that of man in the world of Giotto; the profound reasons that compelled him to liberate his people were the same as those that had compelled Giotto to liberate his own both from the Gothic and from Byzantium. . . ." Nonetheless, it became customary for the spectator to confuse style with naturalistic illusion; and when the means of creating such an illusion had been mastered, the values expressed by art became a function of the subject matter of the picture rather than the outgrowth of a stylistic conquest. "The parallelism between expression and representation—thus, the decisive action of the specific genius of painters on the spectator—ceased when the means of representation had been conquered."

From this point on, the course of Western painting, with some notable exceptions, ceased to be a development of plastic resources and shifted, instead, to refining the expressiveness of the people represented; art, in other words, became theater. It no longer spoke its own language—the language of plastic forms—but began to base its appeal on the drama of gesticulation and the subtlety and complexity of the emotions experienced by the characters in the picture. As Malraux observes, the terms in which Stendhal praises Correggio could be applied, word for word, to a great actress or to the plays of Racine. In this Baroque art of the Counter-Reformation, consciously guided by the Jesuits to make religion sensuously appealing, "painting wished to be a sublime theater"; and while the great Baroque colorists, as Malraux recognizes, "recovered the lyric expression defunct with the stained-glass window," they nonetheless subordinated the specific values of painting to the "rational" expression of sentiments in their personages. Rembrandt, who refused to subordinate painting to people in the *Night Watch* and in his later works, was, significantly, the first "*peintre maudit*," whose creations aroused fierce social opposition.

As a result, this divorce between the plastic language of art and its ability to create the illusion of natural appearance became a fixed feature of Western painting. "The fundamental change in the function of painting"—writes Malraux, summing up this section of his argument— "whose consequences had been Italian eclecticism, then the sentimental '*beau idéal*,' culminated, after Greuze, in the immense cemetery of nineteenth-century academicism: there also, the union of 'tried-and-true' formulas, seasoned from time to time with a dash of *brio*, was placed at the service of an art in which the spectator indifferent to painting played a principal role; except that a historical fiction was substituted for the religious one." This was the final stage in what Malraux calls the "death-pangs of fiction" in the plastic arts. With the triumph of Manet, whose name and work are used by Malraux to symbolize the break between academic and modern art, the plastic arts escaped from the blind alley in which they had been entrapped for so long; and the world of fiction, abandoned by the modern artist, found its proper medium of expression in the movies.[2]

The ideas of Malraux we have sketched so far will, no doubt, seem familiar to those acquainted with the theories of modern art criticism. From defenders of Post-Impressionism like Roger Fry, we have all learned that the subject matter of a work of art, taken by itself, is of no aesthetic importance; that what gives value to a work of art is its "form," or, to use Clive Bell's much-debated term, "significant form." This theory, of course, is a

direct result of what Malraux has called the intellectualization of art. It is the conceptual reflex of our museum-
relationship to culture, which, by sundering works of
art from their organic context, implicitly assumes they
are bound together by some common aesthetic quality
that might as well be called "significant form." But modern art, too, is a product of the same conditions that led
to the triumph of such a museum-culture; and it is no
accident that the chief advocates of modern art, in trying
to define its essential features, should fall back on "significant form" as their last word. Unfortunately, as Roger
Fry admitted in *Vision and Design,* neither he nor Clive
Bell could get beyond "a vague adumbration of the nature of significant form."[3] Without alluding directly to
these English writers, Malraux nonetheless takes up the
problem and, by placing it in a sweeping historical perspective, makes an effort to carry the interpretation of
modern art beyond the point at which Fry had given up.
If the essential feature of modern art is that form—the
language of art, its plastic means and resources—has
suddenly become significant, in what does this significance consist?

Maurice Denis, in his influential book of art criticism,
Théories, wrote that for the modern artist, "before being
a warhorse, a naked woman, or some sort of anecdote, a
picture is essentially a plane surface covered over with
colors assembled in a certain order." Malraux takes this
phrase to mean that painting has ceased to be a means
and has become an end; art has, in other words, become
its own value, instead of subordinating its formal qualities to the expression of some extra-aesthetic value. "After having been a means of access to the sacred, painting
had been a means of transfiguration," Malraux observes;
it was the value of the sacred in the Middle Ages, the

value of transfiguration in terms of the Greco-Roman ideal, which had set the boundaries within which the individuality of the artist had to do its work. But "by its break with fiction, painting was forced to become its own value"; and the result was that modern art sought "a reversal of the relation between the object and the picture—the subordination of the object to the picture." Formal values thus became the dominant concern of the modern artist, in the sense that the world of objects was made subordinate to the plastic equivalents through which each artist strove to create his individual universe. Modern art, then, is defined by Malraux as "the search, through the forms, for an interior schema which then takes—or not—the form of objects, but of which the objects are only the expression."

The freeing of art from extra-aesthetic values incorporated in a particular subject matter has, of course, reached its culmination in modern art; but Hegel, the greatest of modern aestheticians, had already seen the same tendency at work in the dissolution of what he called "romantic" art (the same art which, for Malraux, embodies the value of the "sacred")—the art whose plastic resources were employed to express the transcendental values of Christianity. Once these values ceased to be controlling, once they ceased to furnish the artist—as Hegel writes in his *Vorlesungen über die Aesthetik*—"a content, with which his innermost subjectivity lives in primordial unity," the content of art became a matter of impulse and caprice, depending solely on the artist's subjectivity; and consequently, "without regard for subject matter, the means of representation became ends in themselves, so that the subjective dexterity and employment of artistic means elevated itself to become the objective matter of the art work." And in a sentence that might refer to modern abstract art, although Hegel was actually talking about Dutch *genre* painting, he calls this "as it were, an objective music, a singing in colors." For Hegel's dialectic, naturally, this freedom of the artist had a double aspect. Compared to the great periods when art was an authentic voice for the *Weltanschauung* of an entire culture, the subjectivity of art represented a decline in status. Art was no longer the chosen instrument for expressing the highest values of modern culture—a task which, because of the *Innerlichkeit* of the modern spirit, had now devolved on philosophy. At the same time, Hegel recognized that, in being released from bondage to any particular framework of values, a new world of possibilities had been thrown open to the artist; "every form, as every material, now stood in his service and at his command."

Hegel's ideas have been introduced, at this juncture, to highlight Malraux's conviction that in becoming its own value modern art has reached a historical apotheosis. For while Hegel tried to keep a balance between the positive and negative implications of this tendency, for Malraux only the positive aspect exists—it is an unconditional triumph. Manet and the modern art beginning with him, Malraux believes, "isolated an artistic attitude from the centuries." Instead of turning back to a single past style for inspiration, the modern artist, deluged by the creations of all history, forged a new style based on a unique insight into the essence of art. This insight, briefly expressed, was that "every great artist is a transformer of forms; the new fact was that the modern artist became aware of this; and whoever was aware of it formerly is modern in some way." The art of the past, that is, had transformed the world of forms in keeping with some extra-aesthetic value, whether religious or secular; but the essence of art had only been obscured by its subservience to these extra-aesthetic values; for this essence lay in art's pure function as a transformer of the given world of forms, independently of the extra-aesthetic values that had guided the transformation. Only in modern art, Malraux stresses, has this pure function of art disengaged itself to become the controlling value of a great communal style; and while this style is "perhaps the most intellectual that the history of art has known," Malraux intimates that it may well be, nonetheless, "the greatest style that the Occident has sheltered."

Malraux's specifically aesthetic conclusions, which, in an abstract form, are quite familiar from earlier art criticism, flow directly from this analysis of modern art. If, as modern art has disclosed clearly for the first time, the essence of art is to be a pure transformer of forms, then it is clear that art can in no way be equated with imitation— the artist does not paint what he sees, but transforms what he sees into what he paints. Some of Malraux's most dazzling pages, however, are devoted to proving this point historically. To mention only two instances, he traces the metamorphosis of the sensuously vital forms of Greco-Roman art, brought to India in the wake of Alexander the Great, into the serenely meditative Greco-Buddhist sculpture of Gandhara: then into the lonely, monumental transfixions of the saints in Byzantine mosaics: finally, in the West, into the vibrantly individual portraits that Gothic sculpture, at its height, made out of Greco-Roman idealizations. And in comparing the three versions of El Greco's *Christ Driving the Money-Changers from the Temple*, Malraux brilliantly describes the elimination of *décor*, the shift from conventional modelling to El Greco's flamelike Gothic elongations, the suppression, in the final version, of all that marked the colorful charm and sensuous profusion of the Venetian style. Even though these pages belabor a point that hardly needs to be proven at such length, it would be ungrateful to criticize Malraux's expansiveness when it produces analyses of such scintillating quality.

More important is the metaphysical status attributed to art by Malraux, which also stems from art's function as a pure transformer of a given world of forms. This status, too, is a traditional motif in aesthetics, particularly the aesthetics of German idealism. Throughout history, Malraux tells us, art has torn man away from the world to which he must submit so that he might enter a world which he governs. "All art is a battle against destiny, against the consciousness of what the cosmos holds that is indifferent to man and menacing for him: earth and death." The difference between life and its artistic representation, Malraux argues, is "the suppression of destiny"; and the "eruption of all the arts into the Imaginary Museum suggests to us that all art is an order; that destiny is vanquished in proportion as things are reduced to the human—when the world loses its autonomy." To this central thesis of his book Malraux returns again and again from different angles, with a desperate reiteration that indicates the emotional importance he attaches to it; but there is no point in dealing at length with the variations he plays on this theme. Let us, in concluding this section, simply quote one of his strongest professions of faith in art, where he daringly gives it religious rank.

> The discovery of art, as in every conversion, is the rupture of an anterior relation between man and the world. Creators and amateurs, all those for whom art exists, that is, all those who can be as sensitive to

forms created by it as to the most moving of mortal forms, are distinguished by their faith in a special power of man. They devalue the real as the Christian world devalued it, and as every religious world does. And like the Christians, they devalue it by their faith in a privilege, by the hope that man, and not chaos, carries in himself the source of his eternity.

· · ·

Parallel with the ideas outlined above, there is another current of thought in Malraux that, for a time, accompanies them, providing a menacing undertone to the clear note of joy sounded about modern art. This undertone, which has to do with the influence of primitivism, is abruptly dropped just at the point where it might come into embarrassing conflict with Malraux's contention that modern art is controlled only by a functional value—the pure, transforming nature of art itself—rather than by an extra-aesthetic value springing from the substance of modern culture. Malraux is too honest a mind, too unremitting a sensibility, to disregard the primitive influences on modern art. He writes about this "barbaric Renaissance," as he graphically calls it, with unforgettable expressiveness, and with a full consciousness of the underworld of passion and terror in which primitive art has its roots. Yet he shrinks—or so it seems to me—from trying to test the possible meaning of this influence against his own theory of modern art and prefers instead to let it quietly drop out of sight. Still, before doing so, he tells us enough to reveal the contradiction he no doubt senses but refused to grapple with— the contradiction between the extra-aesthetic values of primitive art and the belief that modern art, strongly influenced by the primitives, obeys only an aesthetic imperative.

Malraux makes his most telling point against himself when he notes, quite acutely, that not all art styles have been welcomed into the Imaginary Museum on an equal footing. Some are kept locked in the storerooms, rather than being hung, along with the others, in the main galleries. The art of Tibet, for instance, which represents imaginary human forms in movement, still has the status of a curio rather than a style; nor have those periods of Chinese or Persian art that express a high degree of "humanist refinement" exercised any lasting influence on modern art. Clearly, a principle of selection has been at work guiding the resurrections that have molded modern art; and this principle, as Malraux puts it negatively, has worked against any art style that might be "what the eighteenth and nineteenth century took for civilized." Positively, it has favored any primitive style that obviously lacked "humanist refinement," or any civilized style from which human values, as distinct from transcendent ones, have been rigorously excluded (Byzantine art, where man was "crushed by God"). Here, then, is evidence that values other than aesthetic have played a decisive role in modern art. "The conflict that opposed modern art to the museum of the nineteenth century" Malraux states incisively, "involved an unconscious questioning of humanist values."

Nor does Malraux have any illusions about the precise import of the questions posed to humanist values by modern art. "From war, a major demon, to the complexes, minor demons, the demonic domain—present more or less subtly in all barbaric arts—has reentered the scene"; and the demonic, far from being humanist, is defined by Malraux as "all that which, in man, aspires to destroy him." Even more, Malraux explicitly links

this return of the demonic with the principle of selection employed by modern art in arranging the Imaginary Museum. "The more the new demons appeared in
Europe, so much the more did European art find its ancestors in cultures that had known the ancient demons."
And the disappearance of perspective in modern art, its
preference for the plane, is not merely a stylistic idio-
syncrasy: "Satan paints only in two dimensions. . . ."
Modern art, being an accusation against the values of its
culture, calls to its aid those other art styles that were also
accusations. "A subterranean dialogue is established between the Royal Portal at Chartres and the great fetishes,
as different as the sound of an accusation that wished
itself a redemption can be from an accusation of despair."
Both Gothic and primitive art, in other words, are united
against the optimism of the Renaissance and its faith in
man (a faith that no longer stirs modern art); for they
looked exclusively to that "part of man which, from the
art of Mesopotamia to medieval art, had wished to transcend him and see in him only the miserable matter of
sacred spectacles." Whether inspired by the demonic or
the divine, these dehumanized styles are suitable ve-
hicles for what Malraux calls "the anti-humanism of our
century."

How, it may well be asked, does Malraux reconcile all
this with his view that modern art is controlled only by
the pure value of art as the transformer of a given world
of forms? The answer is that he fails to do so: he abandons this theme with two irrelevant comments and an
unconvincing assertion. His comments are "that the
photographs of fetishes have as yet invaded neither the
factories nor the farms—nor even the salons," and that,
"however profound the passion for primitivism may be

among certain artists, they are not strangers to the simple desire to extend their ownership." By these somewhat enigmatic phrases, he unexpectedly reduces the influence of primitivism to a personal whim of a few artists; it is no longer a significant historical phenomenon, reflecting a profound shift in the *Weltanschauung* of modern culture. But Malraux feels compelled, nontheless, to juxtapose against this "barbaric Renaissance" another resurrection, whose historical symbols are Piero della Francesca, El Greco, Georges de La Tour, and Vermeer. These painters, now ranked among the greatest, were considered minor or eccentric at the beginning of the century; their elevation, Malraux asserts, is due to the presence in their works of the style that modern art has made its own—the style of "the classicism of our century . . . the domain of works that suggest to us that their creators dominate them." This style "has ordered our Imaginary Museum almost entirely in opposition to the barbaric Renaissance," placing "the art of mastery face to face with that of miracle."

With the exception of El Greco, however, three of the names mentioned by Malraux have had little influence on modern artists, however great their rise in critical estimation; while the influence of El Greco, with his tortured spirituality, in no way conflicts with the predominant non-naturalistic influence of the primitives. Doubtless, as Malraux remarks elsewhere, no style is ever "reborn without metamorphosis"; and it would be premature to conclude—from the influence of dehumanized styles on modern art—that modern culture is totally reverting to the extra-aesthetic values in which these styles have their origin.[4] After all, the artists of the Renaissance did more than merely revive Greco-Roman forms: they brought to them a new sense of the inner life of the spirit, the result of the Christian centuries, which gave these forms an individual poignancy they had never possessed before. Similarly, modern artists are using dehumanized styles—essentially the styles of anonymous collectivities—to express a rampant individualism that gives them an entirely new character. Yet this is quite different from saying that the extra-aesthetic values of these styles have had no part in their influence.

In comparing Greek art with the Near Eastern styles that preceded it, Malraux writes, in a distinction reminiscent of Worringer: "The art of the world reduced to the earth finds its greatest force in its accord with man; the art of the world of eternity and destiny finds this in its disaccord with man—in stylization." Modern art thus is based on a "disaccord with man," or, to use Wilhelm Worringer's description of dehumanized styles, a dualism between man and nature. Out of this dualism springs a need for an absolute source of values, which, as Worringer explains in *Abstraktion und Einfühlung*, finds expression in a dehumanized, abstract style. Herbert Read, the best informed writer in English on modern aesthetics, has accepted Worringer's theory as the "only one that accounts at all adequately for the geometric, abstract nature of various types of art"; and in an epilogue written in 1947 to his book *Art Now*, Read adds: "The humanistic tradition which has prevailed in Europe for four centuries has not only declined; it is dead. . . . Art, in this respect, is merely fulfilling its mirroring function." Modern art, then, has rejected the anthropomorphic values of the Greco-Roman and Renaissance tradition because modern culture, after a lapse of centuries, is once more troubled by "the world of eternity

and destiny"; and this is why the dehumanized styliza-
tions of primitive and transcendental art occupy such a
prominent place in the Imaginary Museum.

. . .

A criticism of Malraux's book confined to this level, however, would fail to touch the vital nerve of his thought,
the powerful metaphysical urgency that is at the root of
his concern for art. It is easy enough to point out his in-
consistencies; somewhat more difficult to show whence
they arise; hardest of all to explain why one must honor
him for championing the very doctrine that is the source
of his intellectual errancy. For at the center of this book
is not a rational construction but a burning faith—Malraux's belief that art, as a pure function in itself, has
a metaphysical status; that it is a "suppression of destiny," a symbol of man's inviolable nobility in the face of
blind, cosmic forces. It is impossible to understand his
evaluation of modern art, and his refusal to acknowledge
that it is influenced by extra-aesthetic values, except
against the background of this belief. For if modern art
were based, as Malraux claims, solely on the essence of
art as a pure transformer of forms, it would be—in this
metaphysical sense—an ultimate wellspring of humanist values to a greater extent than any previous style.
That Malraux passionately wishes modern art to be such
a source of values is hardly ground for criticism; but he
can only make it so at the sacrifice of his own intuitions
and by emptying the notion of art of all concrete cultural
significance.

A similar problem confronts Malraux when, turning
away from modern art, he bravely asserts his metaphysical postulate against the kaleidoscope of historical art
styles. Once again he is forced into a contradiction be-

tween his theory and his perceptions, except that this time, instead of denying that a particular style is controlled by any extra-aesthetic value, he fills out his metaphysical theory by surreptitiously equating it with the values of Greek culture. In doing so, to be sure, Malraux is merely following in the footsteps of other aestheticians who have supported the same metaphysics of art. For, as we have remarked, Malraux's conception of art is more or less traditional in idealistic aesthetics: we can find it in Hegel's chapter on the beauty of nature, where he explains why such beauty is unsatisfactory and must be supplemented by art. Without going into the intricacies of Hegel's system, the explanation, roughly, is that nature, including man himself as a social entity, is not a proper reflection of the freedom of the spirit; only art— a creation of the spirit liberated from the constraints of nature—is a true objectification of the ·spirit's inner autonomy.

While this concept defined the general nature of art in an abstract sense, Hegel was careful to point out that not all styles corresponded with this ideal nature of art to an equal degree. Indeed, it was only in Greek art, and particularly in Greek sculpture, that the metaphysical value of art received its supreme embodiment; this was the highest summit that art could hope to reach. Greek sculpture was the perfect objectification, in sensuous form, of the inner freedom of the human spirit. And despite his eulogy of modern art, we find Malraux contrasting Greek art with the Oriental styles of the Near East in terms that might be translated from Hegel. "In face of the petrified slavery of Asian figures," he writes, "the movement of Greek statues—the first that had known man—is the very symbol of liberty." Elsewhere, after referring to the "irreducible order of death and the stars" in Egyptian art, and the order of "blood" in Assyrian art, Malraux returns to the Greek: "The sacred dance in which the Hellenic figure appears is that of man, finally released from his destiny."

It would be possible to quote many more such passages on Greek art from Malraux, filled with a dithyrambic enthusiasm totally unexpected in a partisan of the moderns; passages which are, perhaps, the first affirmative words written about the Greeks by an important non-academic writer since the turn of the century. What has happened is that Malraux, like Hegel, finds the freedom of man's spirit, the "suppression of destiny," most translucently expressed by Greek art. And it is literally true to say of this style—as Malraux tries to say of art in general—that its creation was "the rupture of an anterior relation between man and the world." For Ernst Cassirer, in his great work on the categories of mythical thought, part of the *Philosophy of Symbolic Forms*, has confirmed the intuitions of Hegel and Malraux about Greek art. Primitive man, Cassirer explains, has no clear consciousness of the *human* as a genus apart and separate from the world of plants and animals; like them, he is immersed in the general life of nature; he feels identity rather than independence. In the figures of his gods, therefore, "the features of God, man, and animal are never sharply distinguished from each other." And Cassirer remarks that mythical thought, by itself, might never have arrived at the creation of a separate category of the human, distinct from the life of nature, if not for the intervention of Greek art. "It was only art which, by helping man to his own image, in a certain sense discovered the specific idea of man." Greek art is truly a "suppression of destiny" in this profound sense, "the unmistakable symptom of a spiritual transformation, a crisis in the development of man's self-consciousness."[5]

No wonder that Malraux, time after time, poses against the glorification of the human in Greek art the dehumanized quality of primitive and transcendental styles, which, rather than suppressing destiny, submit the human in one way or another to an imperious, inhuman cosmos.

With this in mind, we are in a position to understand the inner dialectic by which Malraux's panegyric of modern art reveals itself as a last-ditch defense, whether consciously or not, of the very values whose style modern art has rejected. Malraux's metaphysics springs, unquestionably, from the humanist values of the Greco-Roman tradition; yet he cannot, with the blithe self-confidence of the early nineteenth century, simply assume with Hegel that non-humanist styles are imperfect art. For humanist values, and the style to which they gave birth, no longer provide an "eternal" or "universal" aesthetic standard—as they have done since the Renaissance—on which such a judgment could be based. Malraux's problem, therefore, was to maintain the unity between the nature of art and humanist values, while assimilating non-humanist styles, on a basis of aesthetic equality, into the general conception of art. But how could this be done? Obviously, only by a tour de force—by identifying humanist values, as Malraux does, with the function of artistic creation itself, rather than with any particular style or cultural tradition; and this tour de force is the origin of all Malraux's difficulties. It prevents him, on the one hand, from conceding the extra-aesthetic influences on modern art; while on the other hand, when he talks of Greek art or that of the early Renaissance, he cannot resist the temptation to incorporate his humanist values in the styles that truly express them.

When applied empirically, as we have seen, Malraux's metaphysic leads to inescapable dilemmas; it is impossible for us to accept it on this level; but it is equally impossible not to share the deep concern for the fate of modern culture that is the driving impetus behind Malraux's theoretical convolutions. Malraux vehemently refuses to surrender the identity of art and humanist values, though he cannot shut his eyes to the historical relativism that has shattered, not only aesthetic absolutes, but all others as well. Like Nietzsche, he is rent by the conflict between his need for an absolute and the agonizing intuition that no such absolute exists. And so, again like Nietzsche, he dissolves all distinctions into the affirmation of an absolute *process;* for this is precisely what Nietzsche did in his late metaphysical doctrine of *"der ewigen Wiederkunft des Gleichen"*—the eternal return of the similar. Plunged into the depths of despair and moral nihilism by the recognition that God was dead, and that, this being so, everything was permissible, Nietzsche found a new source of moral values by affirming the absolute process of destiny itself in its eternal recurrence. Only thus could Nietzsche finally say yes to life, and only thus—by affirming the absolute process of artistic creation—can Malraux say yes to modern art.

Notes

1. André Malraux, *Psychologie de l'Art,* 3 vols. (Geneva, 1947–1949). All the quotations are my own translation. This work is also available in an English translation by Stuart Gilbert, 2 vols. (New York, 1949–1950), which was published after my essay was written.

2. One of Malraux's suggestive *aperçus* is that photography, in a greatly accelerated fashion, has acplished an evolution similar to that of Western

art from Giotto through the Baroque. Early photographs have the sculptural immobility that we find in Giotto. Now, however, photography is capable of capturing the most frenzied kind of movement.

3. There is an excellent brief essay by Benedetto Croce linking the arguments over "significant form" and also over "*la poésie pure*" to traditional positions in the history of modern aesthetics. The dispute in nineteenth-century German aesthetics between the followers of Hegel and those of Herbart—the Hegelians championing an aesthetic of content, the Herbartians one of pure form—was, according to Croce, logically identical with the controversies arising out of modern art. Little progress was made in resolving these latter disagreements, Croce believes, because this connection was lost sight of, and the problems, as a result, could not be formulated on the proper philosophical level. Benedetto Croce, *Ultimi Saggi* (Bari, 1948), 201.

4. The dangers even in partial reversion, however, should not be overlooked. It is no accident that, in addition to Malraux, Thomas Mann should also be preoccupied with this dialectic of modern culture, which he dramatized in the musical symbolism of *Dr. Faustus*. See my essay on this novel in *The Widening Gyre* (New Brunswick, N.J., 1963), 131–161.

5. Ernst Cassirer, *The Philosophy of Symbolic Forms*, 3 vols., trans. Ralph Manheim (New Haven, Conn., 1953–1957), 2:195–199.

5

Formal Criticism and Abstract Art

A T first glance, it would be difficult to imagine two books more oppposed than those of Heinrich Wölfflin and Herbert Read.[1] Wölfflin's great work, *Classic Art*, written more than fifty years ago, is a loving analysis of the great masters of the Italian Renaissance; Read's book, *A Philosophy of Modern Art*, is an enthusiastic and impassioned defense of precisely those aspects of modern art that have brought the Renaissance tradition of naturalism into disrepute. Wölfflin praises Leonardo, Raphael, Michelangelo, and Andrea del Sarto for their narrative skill in depicting a motif, the dramatic vividness and expressiveness resulting from their formal clarity; these qualities have become so alien to modern art that Read never once mentions them in the course of his book. Yet, despite this radical opposition, there is nonetheless a hidden unity between these two books; and this unity, once revealed, tells us a good deal about the often subterranean linkages that make up the "climate" of an historical epoch.

Wölfflin wrote his book in the very same years that modern art was breaking with the Renaissance tradition of painting; and however much he loved this tradition, Wölflin was preparing the way for its theoretical supersession. For Wölfflin saw the history of art as the autonomous unfolding of certain formal visual categories. These formal aspects were primarily, though not exclusively, what he sought to define in Renaissance painting; and a critic like Roger Fry, defending modern painting, could later argue that *only* these formal aspects were relevant for art criticism. Wölfflin himself never wrote a line about Post-Impressionist art and would certainly have decried any attempt to push his critical position to this extreme. Yet, whether willingly or not, there is no doubt that much of Wölfflin's enormous influence is the result of this concatenation between his critical interests and the revolutionary development of the plastic arts in modern times.

Heinrich Wölfflin came on the German critical scene at the end of the last century, when academic art-criticism in Germany and elsewhere was completely dominated by positivist assumptions. Scholars had done a great deal of work in classifying art objects and in exploring their historical backgrounds; but there was a growing feeling that, while all this had a good deal to do with history, it had very little to do with art. The historical emphasis, it is true, was justified as a necessary preparation for criticism. But so much energy was absorbed by the former task that none was left over for the latter— and the means very quickly became the end. Protests first arose, as might have been expected, outside academic circles—from, to be exact, a German sculptor named Adolf Hildebrand who wrote a little book called *The Problem of Form*. Hildebrand argued that art was more than merely the expression of its time or of the personality of the individual artist. Art, Hildebrand said, was primarily the creation of certain visual forms; and these forms were the key to the understanding of the individual artwork. In the preface to *Classic Art*, Wölfflin calls Hildebrand's work "a refreshing shower upon parched earth"; and he rejects historicism for exactly the same reason as Hildebrand—because "the minor relationships are made the chief things, and the artistic content, which follows its own inner laws, is ignored."

Wölfflin's emphasis on "the artistic content, which follows its own inner laws" explains the revolutionary impact of *Classic Art*. There is perhaps no other period in the history of art about which we are so well informed as the Italian Renaissance; no period in which so many details of the life and work of the greatest artists are a matter of record. And, perhaps for this reason, no other epoch has been so little appreciated and evaluated in artistic terms. The history of Renaissance art has been treated either, after the fashion of Vasari, as a series of biographical anecdotes, or, after the fashion of Walter Pater, as a pretext for the critic to transcribe his emotional reactions. Neither of these approaches, of course, is without merit, and Wölfflin is not only an exacting scholar but—what is far rarer among German *Kunstgeschichtler*—the possessor of a light, limpid, sensitive prose style. Wölfflin, however, places both his knowledge and his literary gifts at the service of his own special interest: the "history of seeing," the formal patterns that constitute the schema within which all artists of the same period seem to work.

In the first half of the book, Wölfflin supplies a running commentary to the greatest works of Leonardo, Michelangelo, Raphael, Fra Bartolommeo, and Andrea del Sarto. Perhaps the best way to suggest his method is to quote his distinction between Giotto and Masaccio, made, by way of introduction, in a prefatory chapter on the Quattrocento. For Giotto, struggling to free himself from Byzantine influences, "everything is still glued together; he superimposes head upon head, without allowing himself sufficient space for all the bodies, and the architecture of the background is an uncertain, wavering stage-set without any real relation in scale to the figures." With Masaccio, on the other hand, "for the first time, the picture becomes a stage, constructed by establishing a unified point of vision; a space in which people, trees, houses, have their specific place, which can be geometrically calculated." There is a whole series of other distinctions describing the difference between Giotto's "decorative, flat style" and Masaccio's effort "to render the essence, the corporeality, in the full strength of natural effect"; and the formal evolution of Quattrocento art is contained within the terms of this polarity.

Not the Quattrocento, however, but the first quarter of the Cinquecento—the High Renaissance—is Wölfflin's favorite domain, and it is impossible to do justice to the wealth of subtle observation that he lavishes on the analysis of individual works from this period. But his analysis—whether it concentrates on axial relations or on the symmetry of balancing masses—rarely strays beyond the bounds of formal appreciation. Even when he points out the felicity of a dramatic motif, Wölfflin usually does so to illustrate the High Renaissance skill in harmonizing dramatic action and formal equilibrium. From this point of view, Wölfflin sees the stylistic development from the Quattrocento to the High Renaissance as a movement from proliferating diversity to unified visual expression.

The Quattrocento, he points out, preferred "the flicker of light and shade" and its painters "took delight in caprices and in the multiplicity of small surface modulations;" the High Renaissance favored "a simple style based on large planes" and *its* painters show "a desire for large, still, masses of light and shade." The Quattrocento, "in its attempt to render movement at any cost," searched for complicated poses; the High Renaissance returned "to the elementary vertical and horizontal for major axes of direction, and the primitive full-face and pure profile aspects." Quattrocento groups tend to be conglomerations of isolated figures; the High Renaissance obtains emotional unity by carefully calculated contrasts of expressive attitude and gesture. "The old method of looking at close range," Wölfflin writes, "searching for individual detail and wandering about the picture from part to part is abandoned, and the composition has to make its effect as a whole."

Certain aspects of this evolution, to be sure, may be linked with non-formal correlations; and, in the second part of the book, Wölfflin has two excellent chapters discussing the "new ideals" of High Renaissance art and the "new beauty" that embodied these ideals. For High Renaissance art, through its formal innovations, attained an effect of "classic repose" which corresponded to certain social changes in the period. Quattrocento art was still essentially bourgeois, the product of flourishing and independent mercantile communities; but as we come to the High Renaissance, "a bourgeois art is transformed into an aristocratic one which adopts the distinctive criteria of demeanour and feeling prevalent among the upper classes, and, accordingly, the whole Christian cosmos, saints and heros, had to be re-styled into aristocrats."

The "new beauty," as a result, demanded a weighty, dignified monumentality that Wölfflin discerns everywhere—in the handling of drapery as well as in the proportions of High Renaissance architecture. But while these factors may have affected the content of High Renaissance art, Wölfflin maintains that the formal development ran its own independent course. "The noble gestures of the Cinquecento, its restrained bearing and its spacious and strong beauty characterize the feelings of the generation," he writes in the last chapter of the book; "but all the things we have analyzed so far—clarity of presentation, the desire of the cultivated eye for ever richer and more significant images, until the point is reached where multiplicity can be seen as a coherent unity and the parts can be fused into an inevitable whole (unity)—these are all formal elements which cannot be deduced from the spirit of the age."

So long as we remain within the limits that Wölfflin set for himself, his conclusions are unassailable and his accomplishment cannot be too highly praised. Despite the lapse of time since its first appearance, *Classic Art* is still the finest introduction to the art of the Italian Renaissance and one of the finest introductions extant to art in general. No other modern art critic can compare with Wölfflin in sharpening our sensitivity to visual form; no one else can so well train the eye to "read" a picture as a formal problem for which the artist sought a solution. Wölfflin, it is not too much to say, taught the modern world to "see" the art of the Italian Renaissance with fresh eyes, cleansed from the accretions of centuries of erudition. And, as we read, we feel that his standpoint is that of the artists themselves, who would have recognized their own preoccupations in his pages.

Only if we transgress Wölfflin's own boundaries do we find any grounds for criticism, or rather do we begin to sense the limitations of his method. For Wölfflin tends to write as if the stylistic evolution he traces furnished an unchallenged criterion of artistic value—as if formal progress and artistic worth were interchangeable concepts. The crudities of the Quattrocento are continually contrasted unfavorably with the complex formal triumphs of the High Renaissance, and no other standard of judgment is introduced. Yet one may feel that this point of view is by no means definitive—that an artist

like Giotto, expressively speaking, is far greater and pro-
founder than Andrea del Sarto, despite all the latter's
compositional skill; and that a good deal of Raphael, to a
modern taste, is unbearably sentimental. Wölfflin never
broaches this issue explicitly, but he touches on the question of value-criteria in a revealing footnote. "It is a sign
of an advance in the modern appreciation of pictures,"
he notes, "that the decorative, flat style of Giotto is now
recognized as something of cardinal importance. Yet
one must guard against the bias which would make this
quality the most important thing in art." (I presume this
remark is directed against the pre-Raphaelite vogue of
the late nineteenth century). One must equally guard
against the bias that would make the *opposite* of this
quality the most important thing in art; and in fact,
Wölfflin later used his stylistic concepts exclusively for
analytical purposes. In this early work, however, there
is an unfortunate tendency to blur the distinction between the analytical and the evaluative.

After publishing his *Classic Art*, Wölfflin pursued his
stylistic researches and, in 1915, gave them definitive
form in his epoch-making book *Kunstgeschichtliche Grundbegriffe* (Principles of Art History). Along with Henri
Focillon's *La Vie des formes*, Wölfflin's book is one of the
most important aesthetic works to appear in the first
half of the twentieth century; and its impact on the study
of the plastic arts was instantaneous. Here, Wölfflin concentrated on the development of art from the High Renaissance to the Baroque—from the sixteenth to the
seventeenth century. This evolution, he contended,
could be circumscribed with five pairs of stylistic concepts. For within this period art moved from a *linear
style* to a *painterly style*, from the *plane* to *recession in
depth*, from a *closed form* to an *open form*, from *multiplicity*

to *unity*, and from the *absolute clarity* of a subject seen as a plastic whole to a *relative clarity* in which light and color are no longer subordinate to plastic form. This last distinction, as Wölfflin remarks, is closely linked to the first one between linear and painterly (*malerisch*) and gives the sense of this latter term. Wölfflin illustrates these categories with his usual brilliant perceptiveness; and to those who may wonder why multiplicity is suddenly attributed to the High Renaissance, it should be pointed out that the ascription is relative. High Renaissance art has greater visual unity than the Quattrocento even though, like the latter, it preserved individual plastic contours; but this preservation of contour gives it the appearance of multiplicity compared to the dissolution of plastic form in the relative clarity of the Baroque.

Not only did Wölfflin imply that the order of this evolution was irreversible, but also that it could be used to explain any period in the history of art; and this latter idea evoked a storm of controversy that has not yet died down. This is not the place, however, to discuss the vast amount of learned polemic devoted to Wölfflin's theories. But it is worth noting that in 1933 he published some reflections on his *Grundbegriffe* that are now included in a volume of incidental essays, *Gedanken zur Kunstgeschichte*. For the most part, Wölfflin continues to adhere stubbornly to his position; he does recognize, nonetheless, that the relation of his "immanent" history of seeing to other aspects of history poses a considerable problem.

He concedes,

Our reflections have not been concerned with art in the full meaning of the word, for we have not taken into account a decisive aspect, the world of the material. To this latter world belongs not only the question of what (morphological) forms a century creates in, but also how men feel about themselves and their rational and emotional attitude toward things. The problem, then, reduces itself to whether our history of seeing may truly be called an independent history. And this is clearly not the case. . . . Tied to the material world, [it] has always regulated itself according to the demands of time and race.

Yet Wölfflin ends these reconsiderations with a renewed affirmation of the value of his morphology of forms—and he has every right to do so. Whether or not they are universally applicable, Wölfflin's categories have provided art historians with a conceptual (and perceptual) vocabulary that has led to a new precision in the apprehension of formal aesthetic qualities. And if the function of a great critic is to bring his audience into a more intimate contact with the work of art *qua* work of art, Heinrich Wölfflin is among the greatest critics of modern times.

The juxtaposition of Wölfflin's book on the Italian Renaissance with Herbert Read's *Philosophy of Modern Art* leads to something of a paradox. Wölfflin, dealing with the content-laden art of the Renaissance, rigidly restricts himself to structural form; Read, the zealous champion of an abstract and constructivist art of pure form, devotes a good deal of intellectual ingenuity to justifying its symbolic significance. Each critic, it would seem, is intent on stressing the most recondite aspect of his favorite style. I am afraid, however, that Wölfflin comes off far better in this exercise than Read; for while the formal structures that Wölfflin analyzes are immediately evident, the symbolic value that Read attributes to abstract art is a far more dubious quantity.

Read's book is a collection of essays written on various occasions over the past fifteen years, and Sir Herbert himself apologizes for what "is perhaps a grandiloquent title." Yet the book does contain a philosophy of modern art, if only fragmentarily, and it is Read's great merit that he has never shirked his philosophical responsibility. All too many critics are content to subsist on second-hand scraps of outworn philosophical and aesthetic theories; but Read, throughout a lengthy career, has maintained an invigorating receptivity to currents of thought blowing from all directions. One may sometimes feel, it is true, that he has been a bit too much of a weather vane—but the Anglo-American critical scene would have been far poorer, and far less stimulating, if Herbert Read had not been there to champion the cause of Reason (as he did, with T. S. Eliot, in the Twenties), to throw himself into Marx, Freud, Surrealism, and Anarchism (as he did in the Thirties), and to attempt a synthesis of Existentialism and abstract art (as he appears to be doing in the chief essays in *Philosophy of Modern Art*).

The problem that has long preoccupied Read's attention is, indeed, the basic question for any philosophy of modern art. Since the early years of this century, the plastic arts have experienced one of the great stylistic revolutions of art history—a revolution comparable in scope, though opposite in direction, to the Renaissance development whose formal features Wölfflin so masterfully described. Several essays trace the historical course of this modern movement in art; and, along with Read's earlier book *Art Now*, these are probably the best introduction to the various schools and theories of modern art to have appeared in English. There are also a series of short pieces on individual artists such as Picasso, Paul Klee, Naum Gabo, and Henry Moore, and several more theoretical essays on aesthetic problems. It is from these latter and from scattered remarks in the others that we may deduce Read's philosophical apologia for modern art.

Sir Herbert dedicates his book to Wilhelm Worringer, whom he calls "my esteemed master in the philosophy of art," and Worringer's ideas have contributed no little to shaping Read's views. Worringer is the German art historian who, in a famous work called *Abstraktion und Einfühlung*, devoted himself to studying the historic alternation between organic styles in art, such as the Greek and the Renaissance, and styles tending toward hieratic formalization such as the Egyptian and the Byzantine. For the first time he placed both on an equal footing, and, in so doing, he provided modern art with a pedigree and a rationale. After Worringer, it was no longer possible to look on the development of Western art since the Renaissance as the slow attainment of perfection and to regard any infraction of its canons either as sensationalism or incompetence. It was necessary to recognize that non-organic styles, tending toward abstraction, might have their own validity and their own *raison d'être*.

According to Worringer, this alternation between organic and non-organic styles satisfied diverse metaphysical impulses. Organic styles, according to Read's paraphrase, are "the result of a happy pantheistic relation between man and the outside world, the tendency to abstraction, on the contrary, occurs in races whose attitude to the outside world is the exact contrary of this." Or, as Read puts it elsewhere, "abstraction is the reaction of man confronted with the abyss of nothingness, the expression of an *Angst* which distrusts or renounces the organic principle." It may well be, as Read suggests, that Worringer's ideas had a direct influence on the evolution of modern art through Kandinsky and the *Blaue Reiter* group in Munich; but they served, in any case, to justify and explain the influence on modern art of primitive and hieratic styles.

The modern situation, however, is by no means as simple as the one that Worringer describes. In the present chaos of conflicting schools, every conceivable style has its fervent adherents; the same artist at different periods may create either in a style approximating more closely to realism or to abstraction. In Read's view,

"We seem to have reached a stage of development where an individual choice is possible. . . . Such ambivalence in the artist proves that the human will can intervene as a process in the existential dialectic. The freedom to create is thus to be interpreted as a freedom to affirm and intensify the life-process itself (which would imply a naturalistic art) or as a freedom to create a new order of reality, distinct from the life-processes, but enhancing the independent spiritual powers of man's isolated consciousness (which would imply an abstract and transcendental art).

These are the general outlines of Read's philosophy of modern art, and, as we can see, it leaves the way open for the widest diversity of artistic inspiration. No one would wish to quarrel with this tolerant catholicism of taste; but there is no reason to surrender all critical judgment and to refuse to distinguish between pretension and achievement. One may recognize the metaphysical validity of an art style without blinding oneself to the inherent limitations that narrow its creative scope. And Read, in my view, fails to hold this balance in the case of modern abstract art, i.e., a non-objective art of pure form.

Once the ordinary prejudices against abstract art have been overcome, Read is well aware that the problem of its critical justification begins rather than ends. For the most damning criticism of abstract art is that which finds it sensuously pleasant but expressively trivial and which assigns it only a decorative value. In an earlier work, *Art and Society*, Read himself formulated this point of view as cogently as it has ever been put.

> To arrange form and color in an attractive pattern, undoubtedly requires the exercise of a refined aesthetic sensibility, but once the result was achieved it could not stand comparison, in all that art has meant to humanity, with the highest products of representational art. For these, in addition to a decorative appeal fully as strong as that of any abstract composition, had given the extra values of psychological interest or idealistic fancy.

Read did not accept this judgment in 1937, nor does he accept it now; but it cannot be said that he makes out any convincing case for its revision.

Non-objective art, according to Read, is the purest example of the creation of a "new order of reality" independent of nature, and, as a result, "art in this sense becomes the most precious evidence of freedom." He then correlates non-objective art with Existentialism as a crucial expression of the modern psyche. "We have now reached a stage of relativism in philosophy where it is possible to affirm that reality is in fact subjectivity," he asserts, "which means that the individual has no choice but to construct his own reality, however arbitrary and even 'absurd' that may seem." Even if this parallel were absolutely accurate,[2] however, one might still argue that Read has fallen victim to the genetic fallacy. The possible origins of non-objective art in the present cultural situation do not prove that, as works of art, its products have more than decorative significance. Nor is it sufficient to dismiss this criticism as another example of the problem that arises "whenever the public is confronted with an original or 'difficult' type of art." It is not the difficulty of abstract art but its simplicity that is the gravamen of the present criticism; not that abstract art creates an incomprehensible "new order of reality" but rather that the reality it creates is, with the best will in the world, so threadbare and so poverty-stricken.

And when Herbert Read, with his usual honesty, tries to come to grips with the "new order of reality" expressed by abstract art, the result is a deplorable intellectual chaos. Writing of the constructivism of Naum Gabo and Antoine Pevsner and referring in passing to the neo-plasticism of Mondrian, Read explains:

> The particular vision of reality common to the constructivism of Pevsner and Gabo is derived, not from the superficial aspects of a mechanized civilization, nor from the reduction of visual data to their "cubic planes" or "plastic values" (all these activities being merely variations of a naturalistic art), but from an insight into the structural processes of the physical universe as revealed by modern science.

Elsewhere, Read describes such art as "an aesthetic revelation of the elements of reality—that is to say . . . a description or concrete representation of the elements of space and time."

It is difficult to understand why, if non-objective art creates a *new* order of reality, this order should suddenly turn out to be that of modern science. If it is true, as Read maintains, that "the best preparation for the appreciation of constructivist art is a study of Whitehead or Schrödinger," this would be the clearest proof for the very opposite of Read's thesis: namely, that there is nothing new about the order of reality created by this style, which thus cannot serve as a symbol for the capacity of human freedom to create independently of nature. Moreover, it is even more difficult to understand how one can possibly give a *concrete* representation of the elements of space and time. Even if we accept Kant's view that space and time are forms of sensuous intuition, these forms in themselves have no sensuous equivalents; it is nothing but mumbo-jumbo to talk of representing them or their elements. And Kant's forms, after all, were based on old-fashioned Newtonian concepts that still had some relation to sensuous perception. Modern art presumably will have nothing to do with anything less than Einsteinian spacetime, which not only cannot be perceived but actually violates the conditions of sensuous perception—the conditions within which all art destined for human beings must remain.

In the face of assertions such as these, one can only maintain that what we *see* when we look at a Constructivist object appears to be an attractively streamlined shape; what we *see* when we look at a neo-plasticist painting appears to be a more or less harmonious decorative pattern. These tell us nothing more about space and time or about "pure reality" than the shape or decorative pattern on a Mesopotamian pot. And one begins to feel very much like Hans Christian Andersen's little boy, who could only keep repeating that, whatever anybody else might think, it was clear as day that the Emperor had no clothes. But perhaps the argument from authority will be more convincing than the argument from common sense, and I can only appeal to someone not unfamiliar with these matters—Picasso. "The idea of research," he once remarked, "has often led painting into error and forced the artist into fruitless lucubrations. This is perhaps the main fault of modern art. The spirit of inquiry has poisoned all those who do not fully grasp the positive and fundamental elements of modern art, for it has led them to wish to paint the invisible and therefore the unpaintable."

I have no desire, however, to end this discussion of non-objective art on a negative note. In *Art and Society*, Herbert Read defended abstract art on what seems to me entirely legitimate grounds—as a necessary and indispensable aid to architecture and the industrial arts. He argued that the practice of non-objective art led to "a heightened sensibility to the purity of form, the economy of means, and the relevance of color," and this is incontestably true. The example of non-objective art has transformed the applied arts in a manner that can only be applauded, and one would have imagined that non-objective artists and their admirers would be satisfied with this considerable triumph. Unfortunately, this does not seem to have been the case: Read now speaks contemptuously of "cubist wallpapers, cubist linoleum, cubist lamp-shades, cubist electric fittings. . . ." One can only regret that, in attributing to abstract art an invisible symbolic ballast, Herbert Read should thus have been led to deprecate its great positive contribution to the aesthetic sensibility of the modern era.[3]

Notes

1. Heinrich Wölfflin, *Classic Art*, trans. Peter and Linda Murray (London, 1952); Herbert Read, *A Philosophy of Modern Art* (New York, 1953).
2. "Heidegger and Sartre . . . are, profoundly, ontol-

ogists: they aim at constructing a 'science of things.' This purpose is particularly marked in Heidegger, but Sartre has not disavowed it and *L'Etre et le Néant* officially claims to be an ontology. These two ontologies are 'phenomenological,' but this changes nothing as regards their nature as a universal science, that is, applicable to the universality of being and valid for the universality of mankind." Régis Jolivet, *Les doctrines existentialistes de Kierkegaard à J. P. Sartre* (Abbaye de Saint Wandrille, 1948), 15.

3. The issue raised in these last remarks about abstract art have by no means lost its relevance, and the same question keeps recurring. In a recent (March 1989) article, it is put by Hilton Kramer in relation to a new book about Mark Rothko. Although considered one of the greatest of abstract artists, Rothko himself preferred not to be called an abstract painter; and the author of the book about him discovers all sorts of "traces" of earlier figurative art in his canvases—"traces" that, at least to the unaided eye, are not discernible at all. "Which, at the very least," as Kramer writes, "raises the question of what an abstract painting is. Is it an art in which we can find "traces" of whatever our hearts and minds and the fashionable methodologies of academic study may wish us to find, or does what can be seen—and not seen—in the paintings place a limit on what can be said to be present in the painting?" Hilton Kramer, "Was Rothko an abstract painter?" *The New Criterion* 7 (March 1989), 3.

6

E.H. Gombrich:
The Language of Art

T H E Bollingen series of lectures in the National Gallery of Art in Washington have been responsible for some of the most important works in art and aesthetics to have appeared in the past half-century. Jacques Maritain's *Creative Art and Intuition,* Sir Kenneth Clark's *The Nude,* Étienne Gilson's *Painting and Reality*—all have emerged as the product of the invitations to participate in this series. E. H. Gombrich's *Art and Illusion* is still another contribution to this illustrious roster, which sets a very high standard indeed; and his extremely able work, though quite different in kind from its predecessors, is fully equal to them in value.[1]

Gombrich can hardly compete with Maritain's intimate familiarity and sympathy with the modern avant-garde sensibility; nor does he possess Sir Kenneth's historical penetration and stylistic brilliance or Gilson's philosophical depth. But he does have a vast and detailed knowledge of the practice of art as a discipline and a welcome curiosity about the possible relation of the most recent psychology to the problem of artistic representation. Indeed, the greatest merit of Gombrich's book is that he finally succeeds in making experimental psychology seem really helpful about art, rather than, as in the past, merely pretentiously irrelevant.

The great question to which Gombrich addresses himself is that of stylistic change. Why does art have a history? Why, in other words, are there so many differing ways of representing the world when all men presumably possess the same ocular apparatus? This apparently naive question, which disconcertingly gets to the heart of the matter, has usually been answered in terms of cultural history—of what the Germans, who have given most attention to this problem, call *Geistesgeschichte*. The great modern masters of art history—Aloís Riegl, Max Dvořák, Wilhelm Worringer, Erwin Panofsky—tended to explain shifts in style by refined versions of the Hegelian idea of zeitgeist. All manifestations of a culture were somehow linked together; and art styles were seen as one part of a complex whose ultimate explanation was located in the evolution of racial, religious, or metaphysical categories (a Marxist would of course locate this explanation in social-economic categories).

Gombrich, however, who left his native Vienna for England as a refugee, and who, when the book appeared, was head of the Warburg Institute in London, has an understandable antipathy to such doctrines; their misuse by Spengler and Nazi-influenced writers in his own field are still all too fresh in his memory. "By inculcating the habit of talking in terms of 'collectives,' or 'mankind,' 'races,' or 'ages,' [they] weaken resistance to totalitarian habits of mind." Like K. R. Popper, whose influence on his thought he gratefully acknowledges, Gombrich is a determined opponent of all such historical "mythologies." And one of the purposes of his book is to substitute a more scientific, psychological explanation for "some grandiose scheme of evolution" of the type advocated by his predecessors.

So far as this intention forms the polemical thread of Gombrich's discourse, he seems to me to misunderstand his own point of view. In reality, he is arguing at cross-purposes with his opponents—as he admits in a tell-tale sentence in his last chapter. "The purpose of this book" he writes, "is to explain why art has a history, not why its history developed in one direction rather than another." But if this is true, then Gombrich is not offering any alternative to the theories he rejects. For the problem they attempted to solve was precisely this latter one of the *direction* of stylistic change, not the sheer fact of change itself. The psychology of perception, as Gombrich amply demonstrates, can illuminate the fact of change because it proves that "reality" may be "read" in many different ways; but it offers no answer to the question of why certain civilizations preferred certain readings of visual experience. And when Gombrich addresses himself directly to this latter problem, he is forced (though in an evasive and backhanded way) to fall back on the very type of explanation that he deplores theoretically.

A good example is provided by Gombrich's reflections on the "Greek miracle," i.e., the achievement of lifelike representation in Greek sculpture and vase-painting after centuries of Egyptian and Mesopotamian immobility. He rejects all "spurious explanations" of this development based on vague notions of "the evolution of mankind" or "the spirit of the Greeks." Instead, he appeals to the far more "intelligible" idea of the relations of function and form. "May not the conceptual, diagrammatic character of Egyptian images which has so often been described have as much to do with the function of these images as with the hypothetical 'mentality' of the Egyptians?" So far so good: but what is this function? The Egyptian sculptor, Gombrich writes,

could lay claim to the famous appellation of "one who keeps alive." His images weave a spell to enforce eternity. . . . Only the complete embodiment of the typical in its most lasting and changeless form could

assure the *magic validity* of these pictographs for the
"watcher" who could here see both his past and his
eternal future removed from the flux of time. [Italics
added.]

One can only wonder at the failure of Gombrich to realize that he is here defining "function" in terms of the
"hypothetical mentality" of the Egyptian—or rather, in
terms of Egyptian religion. And his reference to the
"magic validity" of the Egyptian image surely refers to a
stage in the "evolution of mankind," especially since
Gombrich attributes the development of Greek art to the
rise of the idea of "fiction," i.e., a divorce between the
image and the "truth" of what it represents. The Greek
relation to the image was no longer magical, and thus
the Greek artist had a freedom to experiment previously
unknown in the history of culture.

Gombrich himself concedes that "the story of the gradual emancipation of conscious fiction from myth and
moral parable . . . could not be treated in isolation from
the rise of critical reason in Greek culture." And so here
we return to the zeitgeist again, rising like a phoenix
from the ashes in which Gombrich's "science" was supposed to immolate it forever!

All this should be enough to prove that the course of
intellectual history cannot be reversed and that it is impossible to reject the insights of historicism—no matter
how susceptible they may be to perversion or how tau-
tological they may become if not carefully handled. After
all, we do not reject medicine because of the horrible experiments carried on in Hitler's concentration camps to
determine the threshold of life or experimental psychology because it comes in very handy for brainwashing.

It would be totally unfair, though, to give the impres-

sion that the bulk of Gombrich's book is taken up with
this unsuccessful polemic. Quite the contrary is the case.
The burden of his massive erudition, which he carries
with commendable lightness, is brought to bear on the
problem of imitation and illusion; it is here that he makes
his most significant and valuable contribution. Modern
art has rejected the whole realm of representation, illusion, or mimesis (whatever we wish to call it) as of no
interest and, indeed, as positively unaesthetic. But this
view, Gombrich argues very convincingly, is based on a
false psychology; the whole notion of "representation"
as a passive registering of visual impressions is non-
sense. His thesis, in brief, is that the art of representation
does not involve reproduction as much as translation. It
is based on finding a set of equivalents whose relationship to each other becomes a medium through which the
artist filters what we call "reality."

"Everything points to the conclusion," he writes, "that
the phrase 'the language of art' is more than a loose
metaphor, that even to describe the visible world in images we need a developed system of schemata. . . . All
art originates in the human mind, in our reactions to the
world rather than in the visible world itself, and it is precisely because all art is 'conceptual' that all representa-
tions are recognizable by their style." This conclusion,
which of course has been a commonplace of idealist aesthetics for almost a century (Hegel rejected the idea of
art as imitation), is now in line with the modern psychology of perception and vision; for this latter stresses
the role of interpretation and active collaboration on the
part of the mind in the process of seeing. We read visual
clues largely in terms of what we have come to expect, in
terms of our mental set, just as we hear garbled words
in terms of the language with which we are familiar.

Each artist who creates a new set of such terms, and who trains us to read "reality" in a different way, is thus literally increasing the richness of our knowledge of the world. This explains the enthusiasm, somewhat baffling in our own day, of such writers as Pliny and Vasari over the first triumphs of illusion in art and also the familiar but puzzling phenomenon that, after immersing ourself in the work of a particular artist or style, we begin to find, as Oscar Wilde put it, that nature imitates art.

It is from this point of view that Gombrich gives us a fascinating, richly documented, and frequently amusing discussion of the role of stereotype, convention, and tradition in the formation of styles. Everywhere he demonstrates the tenacity of schemata handed down through generations of drawing manuals and employed even by such advocates of back-to-nature painting as Constable. Nor is it only the artist for whom schemata are important; they are also the key to what Gombrich calls "the beholder's share." Perception is based on expectation, and the tacit collaboration between the artist and his audience is in this respect of first importance. The creation of illusion cannot be accomplished unless the beholder projects into the picture what the artist has only hinted at in terms of a convention within which the picture has to be read. One of the constantly recurring fallacies of art criticism is to confuse each successive set of such conventions with "nature" and to blur the distinction between literal imitation and the invention of new equivalences. Strictly speaking, from Gombrich's point of view, there is no such thing as "imitation" at all. From this unusual and, so far as my knowledge goes, original position, he rejects the whole Platonic criticism of art developed in *The Republic*.

Most of Gombrich's book is devoted to exploring the fine points of this language of art with a wealth of illustrations from the most diverse fields—including the delightful work of the father of the comic strip, Rodolphe Töpffer. Indeed, so many problems are raised in passing that it is impossible to do more here than touch on a few of the most important. One such is the idea that art took its root in the process of projection, i.e., the reading of rocks, cloud formations and other natural phenomena in terms of familiar shapes. This was suggested in the Renaissance by Leon Battista Alberti (and indirectly by Leonardo); it links up, as Gombrich points out, with the psychological technique of the Rorschach test. Another interesting idea deals with the rise of modern art. Gombrich attributes this, curiously enough, to a clash between the pursuit of perfect illusion and the inherent ambiguity of all vision. Identical shapes on a plane, for example, will seem to vary in size as a result of our knowledge of the size-distance relationship; and this "ambiguity of the canvas destroys the artist's control over his elements . . . this is the real explanation for the revulsion against illusionism that set in at the very time when its means were perfected. They were found to be inartistic, they militated against visual harmonies."

This is suggestive if not very convincing. One suspects that the invention of the camera had more to do with the revolt against illusionism than the vagaries of "natural" sight used by Gombrich to illustrate his contention. Here Gombrich actually sticks to psychology, without smuggling in the zeitgeist, in trying to explain the direction of stylistic change; and the weakness of his explanation—the obvious disparity between imputed cause and known effect—is all too glaring. More persuasive is his contention that modern abstract art, which uses colors and forms to evoke feelings rather than images, still faces the old problem of equivalences in a new way. "Can the world of the mind, of the dream, be explored by experiments that result in accepted conventions as was the world of the waking eye?"

Psychology shows that there is an astonishing amount of agreement among people asked to classify apparently meaningless reactions to things within a limited set of alternatives—for example, whether a sound is ping or pong. This suggests that some sort of conventions *can* be established in abstract art, especially within the controlling context of the work of any individual artist. The ultimate question, however, is whether forms and colors can move us as directly and intensely as music or compete with the richness and complexity of words in expressing the world of the mind. If not, as seems to be the case, then one can only conclude—though Gombrich does not do so himself—that abstract art has wandered up a blind (though highly decorative) alley in abandoning any connection with the waking eye.

In the light of Gombrich's sniping at "grandiose" theories of stylistic change, it is amusing to see how often he acknowledges the concurrence of his own conclusions with those of André Malraux. On the appearance of Malraux's *Voices of Silence*, Gombrich wrote a damning review in which, with a surprising lack of logic, he accused Malraux of being both an ignoramus and a plagiarist of scholarly sources at the same time.[2] Nonetheless, though somewhat grudgingly, Gombrich now concedes that his own ideas on the tenacity and importance of convention, tradition, and schemata were anticipated by Malraux. "Malraux knows," he writes, "that art is born of art, not of nature." Indeed, what Gombrich has really done is to give a psychological explanation for the grip of stylistic tradition in art history. This provides an indispensable supplement to Malraux's emphasis on the creativity of the great genius, whose function consists precisely in breaking this grip and inventing a new schema.

Far from being opposed, the work of the two writers thus dovetails very neatly; and the same is true of an earlier writer like Riegl, whom Gombrich sets out specifically to refute. There is no essential contradiction between Gombrich's account of vision as a selective, purposive process and Riegl's famous idea of *Kunstwollen*, i.e., the idea that styles are not a mere mechanical product of a certain level of technical skill but the result of a different way of "seeing" the world in terms of a cultural tradition. In fact, Gombrich has now given this theory an important grounding in scientific psychology; he has not by any means replaced it, as he appears to believe. For while we must certainly discard all of Riegl's racial and biological explanations for the rise and alternation of such traditions, it is only by a more sober, exact, and judicious analysis of cultural "totalities" that we can hope to come closer to answering the questions that he raised.

Postscript: 1989

Gombrich's book has lately been at the center of a quarrel over the question of convention in art that arises from the recent interest in codes and semiotic systems as the basis of all cultural communication. His pioneering emphasis on the active role of the human mind, or on the human perceptual apparatus, in shaping images of "reality" in the visual arts—what he called "the beholder's share"—was eagerly greeted as confirmation of the view that art should not be thought to have any specifically mimetic function whatever but was merely a congeries of codes. An extreme proponent of this position is Nelson Goodman, who has written in Languages of Art *(1968), that "realistic representation . . . depends not upon imitation or illusion or information but on inculcation. Almost any picture may represent almost anything; that is, given picture and object there is usually a system of representation, a plan of correlation, under which the picture represents the object."*

Gombrich, however, now refuses to accept the idea that the realism or naturalism that characterizes Western art, developed out of the Greco-Roman tradition, is merely a convention like any other. He has more recently argued that it is grounded in the natural biological needs of the human organism to orient itself and to function in space for purposes of self-preservation. This argument has itself been attacked as confusing and contradictory, and in my opinion with much validity.

This is not the place to discuss the various positions pro and con, or to go into all the extremely complicated issues that have been raised in the debate. But I think that much of Gombrich's backing and filling arises from the same problem that I pointed out in my review. His opposition to the notion that all styles are conventions rooted in cultural totalities stems from his deep-rooted antipathy to historicism and his aim of replacing it by a more "scientific" approach to the phenomena of art. Actually, as W. J. T. Mitchell has quite convincingly argued, after a close scrutiny of Gombrich's reasoning, "the entire range of images [still] remains within the realm of convention, but some conventions are for some purpose ('realism,' say) and some for other purposes (religious inspiration, for instance). 'Nature' is not antithetical to convention, but is simply a figure for a special kind of convention—the kind found in a postcard and, to a lesser extent perhaps, in the Mona Lisa."[3] *One may agree with Gombrich that the Western tradition of art comes closer than any other to approximating the natural, unaided vision of biological man; but it has only done so after a long struggle, and certainly on the basis of extremely complicated conventions motivated by determinate cultural choices.*

Notes

1. Ernst H. Gombrich, *Art and Illusion* (New York, 1960).
2. This review, "André Malraux and the Crisis of Expressionism," first appeared in *The Burlington Magazine* (December 1954) and was then reprinted in *Meditations on a Hobby Horse* (London & New York, 1963). Two quotations will illustrate my point. "There is no evidence that Malraux had done a day's consecutive reading in a library or that he has ever tried to hunt up a new fact." A page and a half later: "The opening makes effective use of an idea of Julius von Schlosser's who, at the turn of the century, analyzed *Die Genesis der mittelalterlichen Kunstanschauung* by comparing classical coins with their transformations at the hands of barbarians. There follows a chapter on early Christian art, much on the lines of Dvořák's paper on the Catacomb paintings, while the evaluation of medieval sculpture is reminiscent of Worringer. Indeed there is very little that is new in these pages on late antique and medieval art . . ." One can only assume, if Malraux did not spend any time in a library, that he must have done his reading at home.

   The review dates from 1954; *Art and Illusion* was published in 1960; in the preface to *Meditations on a*

Hobby Horse, Gombrich remarks that his "reprinting of a critical analysis" of Malraux's book "should not obscure my respect for many of its insights." A headnote or endnote would have better repaired the damage.

3. Ernst H. Gombrich, "Image and Code: Scope and Limits of Conventionalism in Pictorial Representation," in *Image and Code,* ed. Wendy Steiner (Ann Arbor, Mich., 1981), 11–42; W. J. T. Mitchell, *Iconology* (Chicago, Ill., 1986), 83.

Index